# Winning Snooker with Eddie Charlton

# Winning Snooker

## WITH

# EDDIE CHARLTON

M

*I dedicate this book to my dear wife, Gloria, who has had the patience to allow me to proceed with my chosen career.*

*With fond memories, and many thanks, to my dear Grandparents who launched me on my way, to my Mother and Father who kept me at it, to two great friends for their understanding and assistance through my career, Mr Rowley Hodgson and Mr A. J. Chown.*

*Finally to my hard working secretary, Robyn Richardson. Without her effort and co-operation the book may not have been written, at least as quickly. I thank all these beautiful people.*

ISBN 0 333 21063 8

First published in Great Britain 1976 by
MACMILLAN LONDON LIMITED
London and Basingstoke
Associated companies in New York,
Toronto, Dublin, Melbourne,
Johannesburg and Delhi

Filmset by Trade Composition, Melbourne
Printed in Australia at The Griffin Press, Adelaide.

# Contents

Author's note:

Although metric measurement is with us I have deliberately retained imperial measurements in my text, as I believe, at this stage that most readers can more readily relate to them. In a game where a precise understanding of measurement is needed I have not wanted to create any confusion in the reader's mind.

# Foreword

Since Eddie Charlton joined the professional ranks of snooker he has dominated the snooker scene in Australia. Not only that, but he has made a great impression in the whole snooker-playing world. Twice he has been runner up in the world's professional championship, and twice he has won the popular BBC television series *Pot Black*. At the time of writing, he also holds the break record in the series of 110.

Dedicated as he is to practice and to keeping fit, there is no reason why he should not be the world's professional champion before very long. A useful billiards player, he would be the first to admit that his fellow countryman, the late Walter Lindrum, was the greatest ever—I thought so too.

It wasn't easy for Eddie in his early days and no one knows better than I the amount of work that must be done to reach the top-ranking handful of players in the world. Always immaculately dressed, he is a most likeable fellow and a great credit to snooker, and, probably more important still, a great sportsman too.

In my opinion his stance and cue action is the finest in the game. Follow Eddie in his book *Winning Snooker* and anyone must improve his game. The photographs are of tremendous interest and his explanations will not only provide excellent reading but will be absorbingly instructive to all followers of snooker.

If I have one criticism to make it would be that he should add a little more attack in his play. When all is said and done you cannot win games unless you keep the score moving along. Discretion must be applied, but Eddie is such a capable player that more attack must pay good dividends.

*Winning Snooker* covers every aspect of the game and it must be a winner in every way. I wish this book all the success which I feel its author so richly deserves.

Joe Davis

MAY 1976

# My Life with Snooker

I started playing the game of snooker in my grandfather's billiards room as a nine-year old schoolboy. My grandfather introduced me to the game because he was a very keen billiards and snooker man and had been in and around billiards rooms almost all his life. He was a wonderful little man, the best friend I have ever had, and I loved him immensely. It was not difficult for him to get me started on snooker, and to keep me at it. I used to practise long hours and I thought so much of my grandparents that I lived with them for almost seven years. I practised before going to school, during lunch hour, and played for hours and hours in the afternoons and evenings.

My grandfather organized a game for me with the late and great Walter Lindrum, when Walter was playing for the war effort and the Red Cross at Anthony Hordern's big store in Pitt Street, Sydney, in 1940. I was 11 years old. Playing before a crowd of 800-odd people was a great experience. It captured my imagination and I have been caught up by it all ever since.

I played most other sports during my school days into my youth and as a younger man. I played 27 years of football, and had a similar number of years surfing. I trained very hard all the year round. I played cricket, tennis, golf, and was in amateur boxing for about eight years. I had the great experience of boxing four rounds with Dave Sands who, at that time, was the British Commonwealth Middleweight Boxing Champion, as well as the Australian Middleweight, Light-heavyweight and Heavyweight Champion.

I was in an athletic club and that led to my being one of the carriers of the Olympic Torch from Darwin to Melbourne for the Olympic Games. I had a long sporting career and was always busy with various games, but I never did get away from the game of snooker. I travelled to Sydney to play competition games and exhibitions. I joined the Amateur Billiards Association and was fortunate enough to win three amateur snooker titles and one amateur billiards title.

I turned professional in 1960, became very keen on the game around about 1965 and, in 1968, after 22 years of working as an engineering fitter in and around coal mines, I became a full-time snooker professional.

My biggest thrill in the game was winning the Australian Professional Snooker Championship for the first time. I think it was an even bigger thrill than winning the Australian Senior Surfboat Championship, which we won at Coolangatta in 1950.

Winning the World Open Snooker Title against Rex Williams of England at the St George Leagues Club in Sydney in 1968 was another great experience.

My outstanding achievement, I think, in the game was to make a 272 break at snooker. I think it is a record that will stand forever in the game of snooker because of the various things that would have to happen to beat my break. The 272 at snooker came, when I was on tour playing for the Royal N.S.W. Institute for Deaf and Blind

Children, at the Kempsey-Crescent Head Country Club, N.S.W. I had to play two opponents a game of snooker each. I broke the balls in the first frame, made a red into the centre pocket, and cleared the table for a break of 137. My new opponent came to the table, the referee re-racked the balls and I potted a red into the same pocket and cleared the table again a second time for a break of 135, making a world record running break of 272. Neither opponent had a shot.

I don't think I will ever do anything more outstanding than that in the game of snooker, and I don't think anybody else will either. Most of the old time greats that have heard about it have told me that they think it is the most outstanding event that has ever happened on a billiard table. To beat my record, a player would have to be playing different opponents, as I was, to be able to make the two opening breaks. Goodness knows what the odds are against making a red off the break twice, and then clearing two complete frames of snooker balls without allowing your opponent a single shot. My break of 272 is only 22 points below the possible for two complete frames of snooker. I would certainly like to be present to see the break that beats it.

I had another wonderful experience when I was playing Ray Reardon over a long tour of New Zealand (something like 273 frames of snooker). In one afternoon's play in Christchurch, I broke the balls in the very last frame of the session (we had an afternoon and night session to play), and Ray cleared the table, making a break of 139. Frank Holz, the organizer and compere of our tour and a former President of the N.Z. Amateur Billiards Association, checked up during the break between the end of that afternoon session and the evening session and found that Ray had established a record snooker break for competitive play in New Zealand of 139.

That night before commencing the evening's play, Frank announced: 'In the last frame this afternoon, Ray Reardon set a New Zealand record of 139 at snooker for competitive play. Now we are going to see Eddie Charlton beat that break with a break of 140!' Everybody laughed about that, including myself. Well, you would not want to know. Ray broke the balls and I commenced my break. I finished up clearing the table and my break finished exactly on 140 which then re-created a new New Zealand snooker record break for competitive play. Ray spent the rest of the tour telling everybody how he held the New Zealand record for about 2 hours. It was a hard break that I made, and during the building of the break I had to count to see the colours that I would take in order to finish in front of Ray's break of 139. It meant that, when some of my shots did not go the way I wanted, I had to pick the right balls (not necessarily the easiest balls) to at least finish with a break of 140. I managed to do it, and that again was a great thrill for me.

Playing against Warren Simpson in the Australian Matchplay Snooker Championship at Shoalhaven Ex-Servicemen's Club at Nowra in N.S.W., I made a break of 141 which is an all-time Australian record for championship play. That record stands as the N.S.W. record as well, so along with those two, I hold the record breaks in snooker for competitive play in Queensland, Western Australia and Victoria.

I had the great experience of making 110 break on *Pot Black* and that is the highest snooker break ever made in competitive play on television. I have no doubt that

Eddie Charlton with his sons Edward (left) and Michael.
Edward, 22, has recently joined professional snooker ranks while Michael, 14, has had two 100 breaks already.

one day it will be beaten. I like playing television competitions, and television has done so much for our game. When television tournaments come along, I am always very keen to play in them.

Well, from all this background here is my book, *Winning Snooker with Eddie Charlton*. I have not asked any player to do anything that I do not do myself. I have copied the styles of various other players over the years. I have employed the good points that I have seen, in my game, and have dismissed the bad points. I have tried them all, and I only ask people to play snooker the way I play it. I think it is the easiest way to play the game, and if you are keen and dedicated enough to practise the shots shown in my book, time and time again until you perfect them, then you should make a good snooker player.

Merely applying some of the principles I outline may improve your game quickly, but snooker is the most demanding, exacting and difficult ball game played, and if you want to be an outstanding snooker player, then you have got to recognize this before you even start. Be prepared to practise the long hours needed and dedicate yourself to the task of becoming a good snooker player.

Snooker is a wonderful game. It has taken me around the world several times. I have been to the United Kingdom on ten occasions in fact and have played over the whole of that country, in Canada twice and the United States three times. I have played extensive tours through New Zealand, Papua New Guinea, Sri Lanka, India, and I have also played in Malta, Singapore, Hong Kong, Rome, Milan, Genoa and Amsterdam.

I have met some wonderful people in my travels and I have always thoroughly enjoyed the game. I still enjoy the game should I lose a match. The things that I always try to do are play the game well, and leave a good impression wherever I go.

EDDIE CHARLTON
1976

12

11                    1

10         13 ● ABOVE
                        CENTRE         2

9         14 ● DEAD
                        CENTRE         3

          15 ● BELOW
                        CENTRE

8                         4

7                     5

6

# Snooker Terminology

| | |
|---|---|
| LOSING HAZARD | Means to play the cue ball into a pocket after contact with an object ball (in snooker, a foul). |
| WINNING HAZARD | To pocket the object ball with the cue ball. |
| RUN THROUGH | To impart top spin on the cue ball by hitting it above centre so that its forward rotation will enable it to continue after contact on the object ball. |
| STUN THROUGH | To force the cue ball forward at speed in preference to a dead strength 'run through'. |
| STUN SHOT | To hold the cue with a very firm grip, stopping short in your cue delivery when striking the cue ball, i.e. to 'kill' any travel of the cue ball. |
| FORCING SHOT | To strike the cue ball with power. |
| DRAW SHOT | To draw the cue ball back towards the striker after contact with the object ball. |
| SCREW BACK | To cause the cue ball to spin backwards towards the striker after contacting with the object ball. |
| CUT SHOT | The fine cutting (feathering the edge) of the object ball. |
| TO POT | To pocket the object ball. |
| SWERVE SHOT | A shot brought into play when it is necessary to go around one or more balls to contact another. |
| MASSÉ | To be played for the same reason as a swerve shot. A quicker turn is desired when distances from the cue ball to the object ball are not sufficient for a swerve to be played. |
| CUE BALL | White ball – always to be struck with the cue tip. |
| OBJECT BALL | All other balls, i.e. reds and coloureds. |
| BRIDGE | Distance of cue from bridge hand thumb to cue tip. |
| SIDE | Means spin. |
| NAP | Means tiny fibres of wool each fitting into and overlapping |

the other, like scales on a fish. (West of England manufactured top quality cloth – Australian merino wool.)

DOUBLING                When an object ball strikes one or more cushions on its journey to a pocket.

PLANT SHOTS             Means one object ball, on to another object ball.

SNOOKERING              Means to cover the ball on by ball or balls not on.

# Equipment

3

## The Cue

No one can play good snooker if the material is not correct. The cue is of the utmost importance. It should reach (when placed perpendicular on the floor) to 1″ below the shoulder. That applies equally whether the player be 5′ or 6′ in height. The weight should not be less than 16 oz. Many players may prefer a lighter weight, but leading professionals shun anything lighter.

Try and secure your own private cue. The cue should be of a preferred weight, be well balanced and taper from butt end to tip end. I prefer a ⅜″ tip and ferrule size for the full size 2¹⁄₁₆″ snooker balls. Do not, under any circumstances, use a cue that is whippy. Select one that is nearly rigid. If the balance is right, the weight of the cue will be distributed evenly. Try to avoid a cue that is top heavy at the tip end. A well balanced cue has its balance point approximately where the butt points meet the shaft. The weight of the cue is important and should suit the feel of the individual player. For instance, if a player said to me: 'I think I prefer the weight of this 18 oz. cue against the 17 oz. that I just used', I would advise him to play with the 18 oz. cue.

My cue is 55″, weighs 17 oz. and has a ⅜″ tip and ferrule. It has a black ebony butt and an English ash shaft.

## The Tip

To tip your cue, remove old glue from it and dress cue to a level surface by using a sharp, fine file. Use a firm to hard tip, avoiding one that is spongy. There are many good contact glues on the market today. Apply glue to cue and the back of the tip and affix when the glue begins to dry. Squeeze the tip on firmly and evenly. Turn cue upside down and press on an even surface to remove air bubbles, then leave to dry before trimming. When the tip is ready for trimming, use a small piece of sandpaper to remove the rough edges from around the surface (until it is like looking at the end of your forefinger) so that a rounded tip will be striking a round ball. I prefer Elk Master tips.

## The Chalk

I hold my chalk before a heater to dry it and prevent it from greasing the cue ball. When a ball is heavily chalked, it kicks and throws unnatural angles. Use your chalk regularly and lightly as over-caking the tip with chalk prevents the tip from gripping the cue ball correctly, and the action of scrubbing the chalk onto the tip with force only wears away the tip. I prefer green Triangle chalk as it does not mark the cue ball. Both Elk Master tips and Triangle chalk are American products.

# Correct Stance

Unless you are comfortable and theoretically right, you are actually starting from behind scratch. Every part of you, and the cue, must become one perfectly functioning unit.

Stance at the table is tremendously important. Unless you are comfortable and have placed the feet and body so that eye alignment is correct, all that follows will be false, and will cause many errors in your game.

Assuming you are a right-handed player and have placed your cue on the line that you consider will put the pot down, before chinning your cue for the correct stance, look straight down on your cue and make sure that your cue line is passing over your right instep. This ensures two very important things:

    (a) that the cue arm is close to the body,
    (b) that the head will be straight when chinning the cue.

The toe of the right shoe should be turned slightly right of square for comfort, and the right knee should never bend, as it is 'anchored' for steadiness and stability. The left shoe should point towards the line of the shot with the toe of the shoe turned slightly in for comfort. The knee of the left leg does bend, allowing your body balance to be forward over the bent left knee and your body weight should then be felt on your left foot. This is a very important point as most shots in snooker are 'follow throughs' and to cue accurately on 'follow through' shots, your body balance must be forward. The distance between the feet is only governed by height, as what you have to do is comfortably stretch out and chin your cue.

Two points to remember:

1. Assuming that your right foot is correctly under the line of the cue, and you feel a tendency to be off balance either way, then move the left foot either in or out depending on which way you may feel off balance. The right foot is not to be moved from under the cue line, unless you are left with an awkward lie such as leaning over the cushion or using the rest.
2. If, when chinning down your cue, you feel bunched up in the back or shoulders, then widen your feet until you are down chinning the cue, comfortably relaxed.

# 4 – Stance (Side)

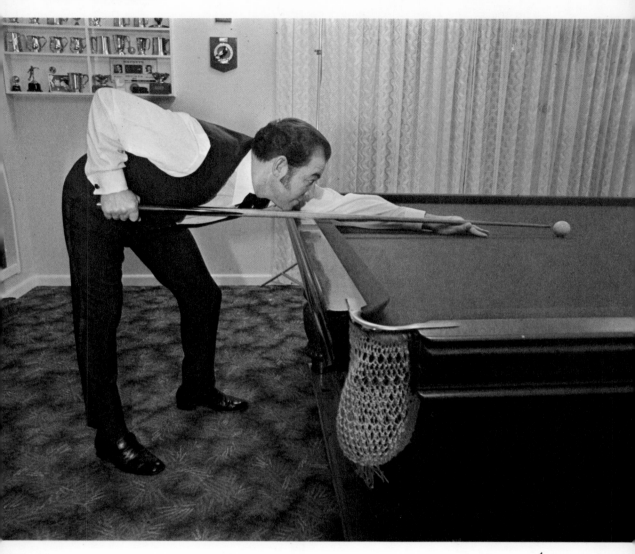

*Note:* *Cue tip* – ½″ from cue ball.

*Cue* – as near to horizontally level as possible.

*Bridge Hand* – firm grip of cloth carrying forward balance.

*Bridge Arm* – as straight as possible always.

*Head* – straight down chinning cue for good rifle-type sighting.

*Cue Hand* – grip cue butt where forehand drops straight from elbow.

*Legs* – comfortably apart – left knee bent, allowing weight to be shared with the bridge hand and right leg. Right leg straight, right instep below cue line.

## 5 – Stance (Feet)

The toe of the right shoe should be turned slightly forward of square for comfort and the right knee should never bend as it is 'anchored' for stance and stability. The left toe should bend towards the line of the shot with the toe of the shoe turned slightly in for comfort. The knee of the left leg does bend allowing your body to be forward over the bent left knee.

5

6

## 6 – Stance (Front)

Aiming at snooker is similar to aiming with a rifle, when the eye must run down the barrel for sighting at the target. So also in snooker must the eye run along the cue for sighting at the object ball. Plate 6 shows my head perfectly straight while chinning the cue. My bridge hand is firm and my bridge arm is straight. My cueing arm hangs straight from the elbow to the cue butt.

## 7 – Stance (Back)

7

In facing the shot and aligning the cue, the right foot, the cue, the cueing arm and the head are all on perfect line. The head is directly above the cue in line of aim. When the time comes to actually strike the cue ball, your eye should be fixed firmly on the object ball.

# Aim

Sighting at snooker is similar to sighting with a rifle. A person, shooting with a rifle, when the time comes to squeeze the trigger, should be sighting at the target. The target in snooker is the object ball. Therefore, when the time comes to deliver the final stroke, the sighting should be on the object ball.

My sighting technique is:

1. To move into position behind the cue ball and position the feet while sighting over the cue ball at an area on the object ball that, when connected on by the cue ball, will send it on line to the pocket.
2. Place the bridge hand and align the cue tip firstly on the area on the cue ball that you intend to strike with the cue tip, and secondly seeing the cue ball on to the object ball that will send it off on line to the pocket.

Having comfortably set your stance, and got down to chinning your cue for good rifle sighting, you are now ready to commence cueing. When you commence cueing, the only moving parts in the whole of your body, other than your cueing arm, are your eyes. Move your eyes to the cue ball to make sure that your cue action is good and that you are in fact going to strike the cue ball where you intend to. When satisfied with that, raise your eyes (not your head) to the object ball, re-checking for a second time that your sighting on to the object ball is still correct. Continuing to cue in a short, flat, smooth, relaxed action, lower your eyes to the cue ball for the second time, re-checking for the second time that you are still going to strike the cue ball in the intended place with the cue tip. Raise your eyes for the third time to the object ball, re-checking for the third time your sighting on to that ball. Then, with your cue tip back to the cue ball, stop your cue for a brief pause, drop your eyes to the cue ball for the third and last time, making sure that your cue tip is still on to the intended area of the cue ball, before raising your eyes to the object ball for the fourth and last time. Concentrating your sighting onto the object ball at this stage, you should be actually staring at the area on the object ball that you intend to contact the cue ball on to, before pulling your cue back and delivering the stroke that sends the cue ball on its journey. This whole procedure has taken no more than 8 – 10 seconds, and your pause in cueing with your cue tip almost up to the cue ball has been quite brief, before delivering the final stroke.

*Remember:* When the time comes to stroke the cue ball, your eyes should be on the object ball. The three important things to have in mind while sighting –

(a) When sighting the object ball, you are saying to yourself, am I hitting this object ball in the right place?

(b) When sighting on the cue ball, am I hitting the cue ball on the area that I intend to with my cue tip?

(c) Finally, while your eyes have been concentrating from the cue ball to the object ball, you always have the feeling in mind regarding your cueing arm, as to how hard or how soft you are going to play the shot.

## 8 – Aim (Cue and Object Ball)

8

I have set up a shot that is just one of the many angles which occur in the game of snooker. Having set my stance and aligned my cue from the cue ball on to the object ball, I am now ready to commence cueing. You are seeing the shot lined up as I see it. I see the cue ball on a continuation of the line of my cue, against the object ball where the second cue ball is now.

## 9 –Aim (Object and Five Cue Balls)

The blue ball is to be pocketed into the centre pocket with any one of five cue balls set up at different angles. On attempting to pocket the blue ball on each of five occasions using a different cue ball for each shot, the point to be remembered is that every time you move behind a new cue ball, the potting angle is altering, but the contact point never alters. Wherever the cue ball comes from, the one and only correct contact point is the point on the object ball where you see the sixth cue ball.

9

10

## 10 –Aim (Object and One Cue Ball)

This illustration shows the line of the cue to the cue ball, the white line of the cue ball to the object ball, and the red line of the object ball to the pocket. I have placed the second cue ball against the object ball, showing the contact point when the cue ball reached the object ball, sending the object ball on its journey to the pocket.

## 11 −Aim (Object and Two Cue Balls)

Plate 11 shows a second cue ball against the object ball illustrating my previously explained sighting technique of seeing the cue ball on a continuation of the line of my cue against the object ball when contact takes place.

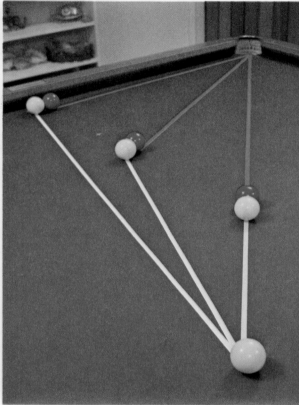

11

12

## 12 −Aim (Three Object and Four Cue Balls)

The picture shows three object and four cue balls, depicting the correct point from one cue ball to all three object balls, all at different angles to the pocket. The three cue balls placed against each of the three object balls show the desired contact point. You will see that the closest object ball is a straight pot (full ball contact). The second object ball is a half ball contact, and the third object ball is a fine cut (feathering the edge).

*23*

# Cueing

Probably the most important point in the whole game of snooker is the correct striking of the cue tip onto the cue ball. There is no instance I can think of where a good cueist would not be a good player.

My aiming technique, if followed as I have laid down, is not at all difficult. With the practice and experience I have to this day, I can say that aiming at snooker does not cause me any concern at all. In fact I would say that if I had a machine to fire the cue ball for me, I would pot every ball I aimed at.

Cueing, however, will always be the art of the game. When I miss shots at snooker it is usually because of my cueing. That is where the human element comes in, and is the reason that, however hard a person may try, however long a person may practise, he cannot pot all the balls all the time.

Shots can be missed when it is not the player's fault! It can happen when a table is not level, allowing balls to run off. The nap on a cloth, running from baulk end to spot end, will turn slow moving balls from their true course, mainly across and against the nap. Again, balls running around on a dirty table can pick up chalk from cue tips which, having attached to a ball or balls, will cause a 'kick' on contact, resulting in the object ball breaking away from the cue ball at an incorrect angle.

These few points I mention are all part of the game, and have to be contended with. To play snooker consistently well, however, you certainly have to practise to develop a good cue action, and then work hard to maintain that action. In my lesson on aiming, you will recall my very important point of watching the object ball when the time comes to strike the cue ball. You may wonder how you can hit the cue ball in the correct place with the cue tip when you are not even watching it.

The answer is, of course, good cueing. My technique is to rely on my solid, comfortable stance, and my good cue action, to finally strike the cue ball at the intended point on its circumference, when I am not watching it. But if you recall I had checked on my cueing at the cue ball *three* times during my address, sighting, and while doing my preliminary cueing movements prior to striking the cue ball.

On moving into my shot, I concentrate on positioning my feet, placing my bridge hand, and aligning my cue – (a) to striking the cue ball where I intend to, and (b) to the area of the object ball that will send that object ball off on its journey towards the pocket.

Having comfortably taken my stance, aligned my cue and my aim, I am now ready to start cueing. With my cue tip approximately ½″ from the cue ball at address, my length of backward stroke will be governed entirely by the power I intend putting into the shot.

Because my power does not come from the *grip* of my cue but, in fact, from the drive of my cueing arm, it stands to reason that if I intend to play a soft stroke, the travel of my cue tip back from the cue ball will be *short*.

Because of the intended soft stroke, my bridge from bridge hand to cue ball would be shorter than normal. Having shortened up in front with my bridge hand, it follows that I will shorten up my gripping point on the butt of my cue with my cueing hand. I play from on, or close to cushions the same way!

In your preliminary cueing movements, you should be aware of your cue finishing its forward stroke ½″ back from the cue ball. Commence your back and forth cueing action in a steady, relaxed, unhurried manner. Keep your cue as horizontally level as possible. The only moving parts of the whole of your body should be your eyes (moving slowly and easily from cue ball to object ball, and back to cue ball as explained in my lesson on Aiming) and your cueing arm.

Your cueing arm is your forearm, wrist and fist, all swinging from your elbow as one unit. Do not develop a wristy action. There should be no wrist action at all, for any shot in snooker, if you follow my advice. There is to be no movement of your cue arm shoulder at all. Your cueing arm is to swing from the elbow only.

Your cue action should be a short, flat, back and forth motion, as relaxed, steady and as slow as you can manage, without losing the nice, smooth rhythm you should continually practise to develop into your technique.

There also is great timing required if you are to become a good cueist. Timing is absolutely essential, otherwise you will never consistently stroke your shots at the right speed. What follows then, of course, is that your intended distance of travel of the cue ball seldom works out as planned. The timing I speak of is between your eyes, and your cueing arm.

The occasions when I play well, which fortunately is most of the time, providing I am not mentally tired from late nights and excessive travelling, are the occasions that I am fresh and keen to play, and can have the three all important fundamentals of snooker working together in my mind and actions at the same time:

1.  While staring at the object ball and saying to myself: 'Yes, my aim is good, and I am going to hit the object ball in the right place to send it to the pocket'.

2.  While staring at the cue ball and saying to myself: 'Yes, my cue action is good, and I am going to strike the cue ball with the tip of my cue where I intend to'.

3.  While the concentration of my mind and eyes have been on the two balls concerned, I have always had the feel of my cue, in stroking back and forth during my preliminary movements, as to exactly how hard or how soft I am going to play the particular shot.

My sighting and cueing technique, from the time my stance was set and cue aligned, has taken 8–10 seconds.

Now, happy with all thoughts on this particular shot, when staring at the object ball for the third time, I stop my cue with the cue tip to within ½″ of the cue ball, for the fraction of a second that it takes to lower my eyes to the cue ball. Then finally making sure that my cue tip is still going to strike the intended area on the cue ball, I raise my eyes back to the intended area on the object ball, and deliver my stroke by pulling back and finally playing forward, and through, the cue ball.

I have found that the slight pause has been invaluable in my play since the great Joe Davis (undefeated World Professional Snooker Champion for twenty years) offered me that advice whilst helping me with my game on my first visit to London in 1968.

Joe and I have become very good friends over the years, and his advice to me on the 'pause' before striking is the best advice ever extended to me during my snooker-playing career.

The importance for me in the pause is that, after playing snooker for lengthy sessions over many frames during our big professional matches, I get mentally tired because of the concentration required. While all thoughts and concentration on this particular shot have been going through my mind and actions, the pause allows me to 'gather' in all those thoughts, steady myself, and actually rally strength before finally playing the stroke.

*When cueing note:*

(a)  The pause takes place with the cue tip up to within ½" of the cue ball – not at the back of the stroke!

(b)  Do not clutch the cue in a stranglehold with your cue hand. As firm a grip as it takes to wave your cue around in the air will suffice. Your power should not come from the grip of your cue, but from the feel, or drive, of your cue arm. If a soft shot is to be played, your cue action is a soft push. (Shorten your bridge, shorten your cue hold, shorten your stroke.)

(c)  If a power shot is to be played, your cue action is a smooth, controlled, rhythmic drive of the cue arm. (Lengthen your bridge – not more than 10" – move your hold position on the cue butt so that your forearm, wrist and fist, drop vertically from your elbow, when the cue tip is ½" from the cue ball.)

## 13 – Cueing (Grip, Taking Hold)

The grip being formed. When taking hold of the cue with the cue hand, you should wrap the fingers and thumb around the butt, thus pulling the butt up into the palm of the hand. Do not clutch or strangle the cue. The cue should lie in the middle pads of the four fingers. The grip is taken with the first two fingers and the thumb only. Your remaining two fingers close on to the butt without gripping.

13

## 14 – Cueing (Grip, Inside View)

Plate 14 shows my cue hand gripping the butt of the cue with the first two fingers and the thumb. The remaining two fingers simply close on the butt. I maintain this grip for practically every shot that I play, as my power comes from the drive of my cueing arm and not from slackening or strengthening my grip.

## 15 – Cueing (Grip, Outside View)

The cue hand is shown taking the cue hold where the hand hangs straight from the elbow.

15

## 16 – Cueing (Grip, Back Stroke)

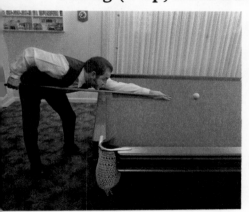

A normal stroke (cue hand to cue ball 10″) at the end of the backswing. My backswing on a normal stroke is 4″. Note the cue is as near to level as possible.

16

## 17 – Cueing (Grip, Forward Stroke)

The cueing arm at the end of the forward stroke. Note my follow through of approximately 5″. My follow through is short compared with most other professional players.

17

## 18 – Cueing (Grip, Back View)

The cue, right elbow, right hand and centre of the head are all on line to the cue ball. Cue hand hanging straight from the elbow allows for relaxed swinging of the cueing arm, and my thumb just brushes my hip while cueing.

18

## 19A – Cueing (Top Spin)

The bridge hand forms a cradle to carry the cue. The body weight is down on the palm of the hand, which grips the cloth with all four finger pads well spread for strength and stability. Forefinger points out to meet a well cocked thumb forming a cradle for the cue to run in. To address the cue tip to the top of the cue ball to apply top spin for follow through shots, note that the knuckles on the bridge hand are high and the cue just clears the cushion rails. Striking point on cue ball for follow through shots, 12 o'clock.

19A

## 19B – Cueing (Centre Striking)

To lower cue tip to the centre of the cue ball, do not lift your back cueing hand and the butt of the cue to get your tip down. To move from 12 o'clock cueing to dead centre striking on the cue ball, simply allow your bridge hand to flatten down, lowering your forefinger knuckle and thumb till cue tip is dead centre on the cue ball. Striking point on the cue ball, 14.

19B

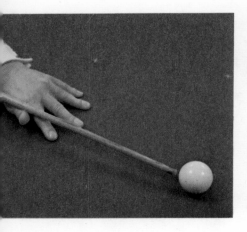

## 19C – Cueing (Stun Shots)

To lower cue tip, below dead centre, for most stun shots again flatten bridge hand, and lower knuckles until cue tip lowers to point 15.

19C

## 19D – Cueing (Deep Screw)

19D

Note bridge hand now. I have turned my wrist to get the weight of my forward balance to the base of my bridge hand thumb, pads of first three fingers, and down to the point of my little finger. The palm of bridge hand is now clear of the table. Base of the thumb is on the cloth, and without raising the back cueing hand at all, cue tip has been successfully lowered to the deep screw striking position on the cue ball. Striking point for deep screw – 6 o'clock. When intending to apply severe back spin for a deep screw shot, remember that you now intend striking down in the mis-cue area. Chalk your tip carefully before attempting this shot and be careful to send your cue through, as previously advised, with a smooth, controlled, rhythmic drive of the cue arm. When attempting this shot a firm grip of the cloth with your bridge hand, and your cue with your cueing hand, is essential.

## 19E – Cueing
### (Bridge Hand, Bridge Arm)

With your body weight forward over your bent left knee on to your bridge hand, you have to support your forward body weight by comfortably setting your bridge arm as straight from your shoulder, to your bridge hand, as is possible depending on the position of the cue ball or any other balls. Having set your stance with your right leg straight (braced against any movement backwards) and your straight left bridge arm (propping onto your bridge hand) those two anchor points will assist greatly in holding you steady against any backward or forward movement, particularly when applying power shots.

19E

## 20 – Cueing (Grip and Head)

Strength of grip for most shots I play is as firm as it takes to move the cue around

20

in the air. Slightly more strength than simply holding the weight of your cue, as now you are controlling your cue, and not your cue controlling you. I am only down in the cue ball addressing position a matter of seconds when the knuckles of my cueing hand turn white with the pressure that is being applied. All four finger pads are around the cue butt. My actual grip, with forearm hanging straight to the gripping position before commencing cueing, is actually being taken with the first two fingers and the thumb only. My back two fingers are simply closed on the cue butt. At the back of my back swing, my two back fingers are still on the butt of the cue, but have allowed the back of the palm of my hand to come off the cue, and the thumb and first two fingers are now in control of the cue. On coming back to strike the cue ball and follow through, my hand has closed allowing four fingers back on to the butt of the cue, but the actual grip is still being maintained by the thumb and first two fingers only.

Do not wrap your thumb around the cue. Allow your thumb to point straight down past the cue towards your right instep, and simply close your straight thumb onto the butt of the cue locking it there between the first two fingers. If you allow your thumb to grip around the cue at all, it will have a strong tendency to pull your cue off line when delivering your stroke.

When down on the stroke passing through the whole aiming and cueing technique, it is extremely important to keep your head absolutely straight and steady. By having my chin down to cue level I have rifle sighting aim and automatically, being a right eye sighter down the cue, my head is perfectly straight. While cueing, I continually feel the cue glancing back and forth under my chin tip. This is a guide for keeping my cue horizontally level, for keeping my head straight and my head, neck and shoulders, absolutely still.

If you feel you are getting head movement on the shot, it could be because you are getting shoulder movement or eye movement during your aiming and cueing activity. You can eliminate shoulder and upper arm movement quite simply by remembering three very important points:

(a) On sighting if you do not let your eyes move from the object ball, particularly on the final stroke, then your head cannot move.

(b) If you are concentrating on swinging your cueing arm from the elbow only, you cannot get upper arm or shoulder movement into the shot.

(c) Do not open and close your cueing hand on the cue butt. Your first two fingers and thumb are always gripping the cue. The back of your palm on your cueing hand, by easing off the cue butt on your backward motion, allows the cue to remain horizontally level during your cueing movements.

# Bridging

When the cue ball is near the rail, always work on my principle of retaining, at all times where possible, the 10″ of bridge previously discussed. If your bridge hand can comfortably be placed down on the bed, between the cushion and cue ball, at the same time retaining 10″ of bridge, then certainly adopt your bridge hand in that position.

It is always a distinct danger on any shot to play a stroke with too long a bridge. With the absolute importance of the accurate striking of the cue ball with the cue tip, it only stands to reason that anyone playing with a bridge of 14″ – 16″, or even 20″, between their bridge hand thumb and the cue ball, simply cannot be sure of where they are striking the cue ball. There is too much cue out from the sliding point on the bridge.

I see some players making shots with two feet of bridge to the cue ball. Do not fall into this category. Stay short, working as often as possible on my advice of a bridge distance of 10″, shot, after shot, after shot!

Because of my very strong feeling regarding this point of correct snooker play, it is always the positioning of my bridge hand that determines the gripping point of my cue hand, onto the cue butt. Having set my bridge, as often as is possible, up to or within 10″ of the cue ball, my cue hand grip will drop to the cue butt where my forearm drops straight from the elbow.

## 21 – Bridging (Out from Cushion)

If insufficient distance between cushion and cue ball prevents the placing of your bridge hand onto the bed of the table for a normal shot, causing an extremely short bridge (shown in later plates), it may suffice to withdraw your bridge hand so that the palm of your bridge hand is up on the edge of the cushion face, with your fingertips down on the bed. If I can adopt this position and only decrease my bridge length to say 9″, I prefer to adopt this bridge hand position than one on top of the cushion rail, where the distance to the cue ball would be too great.

21

## 22 – Bridging (Close to Cushion)

The fingers are placed flat on the rail, and the cue slides between the first two fingers. The fingers close comfortably on the cue shaft to ensure accurate aiming. The thumb beneath the fingers running its length against the cue shaft serves as a guide. This is a good grip for locking the cue when playing a power shot from off cushions. Keep your cue as horizontally level as possible. Again, good cueing will be called for.

22

## 23 – Bridging (On Cushion)

When forced to play straight out from a cushion the cue ball is hard against, it is now impossible to maintain your 10″ of bridge because your bridge hand would not even be on the cushion. I am now forced to move my bridge hand fingers to the very outside edge of the cushion rail. Because my little finger is shorter, I allow it to drop off the rail. By doing this my bridge hand will be back 1″ further. Although I have now placed my three bridge hand fingers to the top outside edge of the cushion rail, I still have my stance set allowing forward balance over my bent left knee, through my straight bridge arm on to my bridge hand fingers. I am forced to shorten my bridge to approximately 5″ and because of shortening my bridge, I shorten my cue hold on the butt of the cue.

Note that my cue hold has now gone forward along the cue butt and that my forearm from elbow to cue hand is forward of vertical. This is one of the few occasions that my cue arm will be forward of vertical. Because I have had to shorten my bridge, I must shorten my stroke. When playing from a position like this, I seldom try to use a forcing shot because I am already in an extremely difficult situation.

To afford myself every chance of playing a good shot, I chalk my cue carefully before adopting this stance. I now allow the butt of the cue to simply cradle in the pads of my four fingers, I relax my grip so that my fingers only are carrying the weight of the cue, and I play most shots with a soft, smooth *push*. I let the cue do the work; I seldom try to play a forcing stroke. I seldom worry overmuch about position for the next shot from this awkward situation because I am content to only pot the ball on this occasion, as my next shot is not going to be as difficult anyway.

A final word of advice on this situation. Try to be careful while cueing, and in delivering your final stroke, not to allow the tip or the bridge of your cue to make contact with the cushion rail. Do not lift your back hand to raise the butt of your cue (thus allowing better striking of the cue tip down onto the cue ball) any more than you have to.

23

24

25

26A

26B

26C

## 24 – Bridging (Across Left)

When forced to play from this position, do not lift the cue butt any higher than you have to. Be careful that your cue tip does not touch the cushion rail before making contact with the cue ball. Having chalked your tip carefully before addressing the shot, try to be content in playing a soft shot which will ensure a smooth delivery.

## 25 – Bridging (Across Right)

Playing off the cushion rail at this angle affords me a much easier opportunity of striking the cue ball correctly than the previous plate showed. Now, being a right-handed player, it is more comfortable to adopt my normal stance, locking my cue along the cushion rail as shown and to use the top of the cushion cloth in this instance as a guide for my cue shaft. I am very careful to have my bridge hand fingers locking the cue so that there will be no movement off the cue line of my cue while, in this instance, cueing across the cushion rail. When cueing along and near to the cushion rail, the next three plates will show my recommended bridge hand positions.

## 26A – Bridging (Along)

I have sufficient room to place my bridge hand in the normal position, however you will note that I have had to bend my elbow to comfortably place my bridge hand in this position, when aligning the cue for the shot to be played.

## 26B – Bridging (Along)

The cue ball even closer to the cushion on a similar shot. Now, with insufficient room to have the palm of bridge hand and all fingers down on to the table, I have allowed two of my fingers to remain in contact on the bed with my forefinger and thumb retaining the normal trough for my cue to run in. My last two fingers are placed up on and along the cushion rail for absolute comfort and stability.

## 26C – Bridging (Along)

The cue ball is now hard against the cushion with the shot to be played along the cushion rail. From this position I cannot retain two fingers on the table bed. Now I adopt the 'boucle' grip by placing my middle finger down on the bed cloth, my last two fingers on top of the cushion rail as before, while making a loop around the cue by my forefinger meeting my thumb. The cue runs against my middle finger and thumb and is held firmly and guided by the inside loop of my forefinger.

# 27A, B – Awkward Bridging (Off Cushions, Right and Wrong)

27A

27B

This is a difficult shot. Only a fraction of the cue ball is there to contact. To make sure of hitting what we can see of it, we have to be careful of our grip and cue action. Most players in this position raise their bridge hand off the cushion rail, so that they have only their fingertips touching, and at the same time address the cue ball with their back cueing hand raised, thus making a downward thrust at the cue ball (pictured). This is very wrong! The possibility of making a miscue is near certain because of the unsteady bridge hand. The awkward cue arm movement that will follow, and worse still, the fact that the player's head will be up off the cue guessing the potting angle instead of sighting it, all contribute to a bad shot. Now, because we are faced with an awkward lie and it is difficult, don't have any false ideas about it: we have to be firm with our approach to this particular lie, and above all we have to have confidence in our ability to handle these cushion shots because they appear quite regularly in games of snooker.

Firstly, chalk your tip, as always, for difficult shots. Secondly, place your bridge hand fingers to the outside edge of the cushion rail (little finger off cushion). Now with the bridge arm stretched out straight, and the bridge hand clamped to the cushion rail, we have a solid bridge and can concentrate on hitting the cue ball well because we can slide the cue back and forth with confidence. In making the stroke, the backward action is *slow* and *short*. The tip of the cue just brushes the edge of the cushion cloth before striking the cue ball. Do not allow the tip to run along the cushion cloth and raise the cue only slightly. This allows the player to have his normal stance and to get his head down over the cue for correct sighting.

Finally, never attempt to play a ball with speed from this position. The speed at which it is possible to play this shot with accuracy is at normal speed or even less. To attempt any more will result in a miscue or applying unintended spin. Recognize that you have a bad lie, and do not attempt anything difficult. By this I mean, put all your concentration into smooth central contact of the cue ball with the cue tip and getting the pot down. Do not make it even more difficult by trying to get perfect position at the same time, because the next shot will probably not be as difficult anyway.

## 27C – Awkward Bridging (Near the Cushion)

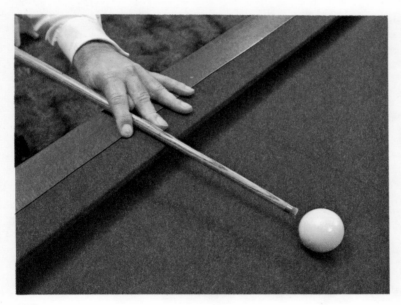

27C

With the cue ball 8″ – 10″ out from the cushion, the 'clamp' bridge would be too far from the ball. This time the bridge is a little nearer the cue ball. We have fingers, palm and the base of the thumb all firmly on the cushion. With the palm flat on the cushion and with the fingers well spread, the cue slides along the channel formed by the knuckle of the forefinger and the thumb. This is not a grip. It is a channel for the cue to run in. Don't let the fingers tighten in on the cue. *Finally*, with this bridge, the cue should be as horizontal as possible, and with practice you can play with any speed you wish.

## 28A – Awkward Bridging (Over Balls)

The action being taken is bridging over balls. You can be confronted with this position at least once in each frame you may play.

Because I realize how easy it is to impart unintentional spin to the cue ball, I always keep in mind not to raise my cue higher than is necessary when clearing the obstructing ball or balls. Grip the cloth with the second, third and small finger pads firmly and allow the body weight to go onto these fingers. Tuck the forefinger up onto the second finger and cock the thumb as in the picture. I consider this is the best bridge possible, where the bridge hand can be put on to the table. It provides a firm bridge hand and allows the maximum height you may require with your bridge fingers, because you are not losing height trying to keep a shorter forefinger to the table.

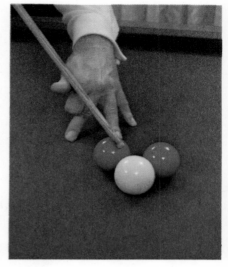

28A

*Points to note in the photograph:* Firstly, that the fingers are well spread for strength and stability. Secondly, there is a great deal of pressure on the finger pads or rather the tips of the fingers. The fingers in fact are bending inwards under the pressure. The thumb is cocked even higher than usual. This adds to the height if extra height is required. A short slow backward action will help keep control. Again, do not attempt anything more than a moderately paced shot. If a higher bridge is required, raise the wrist, taking it more forward. This has the effect of bringing the little finger off the cloth, thus leaving two fingers of the tripod. This is a difficult shot. Take your time over placing the tripod fingers on the cloth. Having done so, brace the left arm out straight. When playing this shot, do not jab at the ball. And do not attempt to scoop at the ball. Confidence will come with practice.

## 28B – Awkward Bridging (Over Balls)

A position forcing me again to play over intervening balls. In this case the cue ball is not as close to the offending object balls as in the previous plate. I can comfortably get down to this shot by placing all four finger pads to the bed of the table with the arm going straight from the shoulder to the finger pads. Grip the cloth firmly with those four finger pads as you do not have the palm of the hand to carry your forward balance.

28B

## 29 – Bridging (Rest)

It is most important to get the head of the rest properly positioned. Most players place it too far away from the cue ball. The distance should not be more than 10". Having taken care to position the cross head on the table so as not to touch any ball, place the rest handle flat on the table, under the line of the cue, and clamp the handle down with the left hand.

Place your feet comfortably apart and square to the table. Body balance is forward through the straight left arm and onto the hand clamping the rest handle onto the table.

29

The grip of thumb and fingers on the butt is moderate, not over-firm and not too light. The flat on the butt of a cue is for the thumb to grip on, underneath the butt, and the first two fingers take their grip on top of the butt. Third and fourth fingers are bent and ride at the side of the butt. The *actual grip* is taken with thumb and first two fingers.

Butt of cue is slightly below level of chin and only raised as high as necessary to strike centrally. Elbow of cueing arm is at same level as butt of cue.

*Cueing action* is a backward push from the elbow, restricting the backswing to as short as 4". Follow through as far as possible and concentrate on striking the cue ball at 14.

## 30 – Bridging (Spider)

Using the spider is somewhat similar to the rest except that because the bridge of the spider is high a stroke is usually made downwards, with only the top of the cue ball to hit. Set yourself comfortably, as with the rest, and play into the ball. A point of importance to remember here is that because you are now playing down onto the cue ball, central vertical striking contact is very important. Striking of the cue tip down on to the cue ball, off the vertical centre line, will have a tendency to spear the cue ball off its course before reaching the object ball. If intending to follow through when using the object ball, striking point is 12 o'clock. If intending to stun the cue ball to a stop, striking point is 14. To attempt a screw shot, the striking point is 6 o'clock. Be content with one of the advised striking positions on the cue ball. You are remaining on the vertical centre line of the cue ball, and will not be risking side on an already difficult shot.

30

## 31A – Follow Through (Straight Pot, Before)

This is a long, near straight pot to be followed through. Notice the cue tip addressing the cue ball at 12 o'clock. Struck here the cue ball will have top spin applied, the required spin essential for following through. The distance the cue ball will follow through the object ball will be determined by the power of the shot, strength of the stroke, or speed of the stroke, whichever way you like to look at it!

31A

31B

## 31B – Follow Through (Straight Pot, After)

Shows the completed follow through position. Having successfully made the shot, I have remained 'down' on the shot following the progress and resulting position of the cue ball.

# Advanced Strokes for Break Building

Break building at snooker is one of the most enjoyable features of this game both for the player and the onlooker.

There is no great secret in being able to keep on potting when building breaks. It is simply a matter of potting with some consistency, positioning the cue ball to allow the next shot to be reasonably easy and, most important, to watch the lie of the object ball and to select the right ball to allow you to carry on the break. To make sizeable breaks regularly you must build up, in addition to some skill at potting, the essential strokes which will enable you to position on to the next ball. I consider the four main strokes in snooker to be the soft stun, the ordinary stun, the soft screw, and the deep screw. The importance of these four strokes for success at snooker is that they are employed stroke after stroke, for at least 90 per cent of my game.

Good players know the angles and paths of the object and cue balls automatically when playing the various shots in billiards and snooker. The learner must watch what is happening to his own strokes and also his opponent's strokes, in an endeavour to catch up to the better player. A good idea is to watch closely what is happening when a professional is playing a match, or better still, when a professional is practising. Notice the pace at which various shots are played, and pay close attention to where the cue ball is being struck by the cue tip, in potting and positional play. Most learners, for instance, are continually going in off, especially into the centre pockets. This is because their lack of angle knowledge, and ball path, lets them down.

## Stun and Screw

In break building, many shots could be potted with plain central striking that would put the pot down, but would most assuredly put an end to the break, because you are not 'on' the next ball. Stun or screw gives much more control and once mastered, allows this shot to be played cleanly, crisply, and usually with enough power to keep the object ball on its straight path. Soft, dribbly shots are much too unreliable. Besides, conditions have to be perfect all the time to play this soft type of game, and there has only to be one small speck of dust or grit on the table for a ball's direction to be diverted.

Stun and screw shots can usually be employed in sending the object ball in with pace and at the same time checking your cue ball to the desired position. The difficult part of using these advanced strokes at snooker is the distinct possibility that the easiest of pots can be missed because of trying to get your cue ball in the most desired position. Even among leading professionals this continually happens.

The cause is the division of concentration. Besides having to put your pot down, you have also to move your cue ball, both in the direction you require and with the distance of travel you intend the cue ball to take in reaching your desired 'position'. Your first and foremost object is to put your pot down. This is much more important than missing the pot to get near-perfect position. By potting your ball you are retaining the strike, keeping your opponent away from the table, and most of all, you are continually building up your score, which is your ultimate aim.

Keep this point in mind: No matter how easy or how difficult a pot may appear, give it all the concentration it deserves.

Stun and screw strokes are for applying reverse spin to the cue ball. By striking the cue ball below centre at 15, you are applying reverse spin. Even though the cue ball goes forward, it is rotating backwards and, when the cue ball gets the impact of the object ball, its forward momentum is halted with a 'bounce-back' effect, and then the reverse spin gets a hold on the nap (cloth) and the ball comes back.

To apply spin to a cue ball effectively, certain conditions are necessary. Probably the most important of these is the tip of the cue itself. A hard, shiny tip will make the task of screwing back so much more difficult, simply because an 'overhard' tip cannot grip the cue ball and apply to it the intended 'twist'.

Balls will not respond to screw and stun if they are old and 'dead'. Balls, besides being chipped and cracked, can lose their resilience, and screw can be hard to impart on balls of unequal weights. Loss of resilience and unequal weights of balls are generally caused by old age.

The surface of a cloth also has quite an effect on a player's ability to play deep screw shots. The newer and heavier a cloth is, then the more it will take spin. A player probably could draw back further on a cloth of medium weight because the nap is fine and will let balls run on further than a heavy nap, but the heavy nap will take spin better.

I have mentioned the above conditions before going onto the various ways of playing stun and screw shots, as I have had to play on poor conditions and I know that many players are forced to do the same. I know how hard screw and stun shots are to make successfully. Bad tables and balls can be a real headache, and besides this, I have watched the average player struggling to play these shots successfully with tips that are allowing him no chance of succeeding.

Perhaps a player can do nothing towards the reconditioning of a table, but every player can own his own cue, have a first-class tip on it, and can chalk the tip as regularly as is necessary to ensure no miscues.

A player has to keep in mind that if he intends to bring the cue ball back, then he has to hit low. *Most players do not do this.* They think they are striking the ball 'low', but their cue action is such that they actually strike the ball in the centre or just below centre, and they only stun the ball to a stop because the necessary back spin has not been applied for the screw shot.

Application of stun and screw, I consider, are the 'Shots of the Game'. I would like to request a closer study of my playing technique so that you, too, can learn to play these shots as confidently as I do. I am sure I can help all interested players with my explanations of these strokes.

Some of the reasons for 'lack of back spin' being achieved are as follows:

(a) Most players try to hit too hard, thus causing cueing errors, especially not getting their cue tip low to the ball.
(b) Striking too low, thus miscueing, or 'jumping' the cue ball.
(c) Instead of a controlled follow through for screw shots, too many employ a jerky, stabbing action that imparts no screw effect whatsoever.

There are many points concerning these strokes that I will cover later on, but to start with we will play all our stun and screw shots by striking 'low' and alternating the power and follow through to achieve our purpose.

Stance is of immense importance with these strokes. Where I normally have a bridge of 10″ for plain central striking of the cue ball, I shorten my bridge to 8″ for the stun and screw shots. Having moved my bridge hand closer to the cue ball to shorten the bridge, I now take a firmer grip of the cloth with the pads of my bridge hand fingers and a firmer grip of the cue with my cueing fingers. Because my bridge is shorter, my gripping position on the cue butt has also shortened up, so that the cueing forearm still hangs straight to the cue butt. The firmer grip of the bridge hand is for extra steadiness, and the firmer grip of the cueing hand is to feel the 'power', and 'grip of the tip', through to the cue ball.

For the screw shot, especially the deep screw, I have to play with some power. I have to be sure of striking as 'low' to the cue ball as I intend to. The firmer grip of bridge and cueing hand is to make my task easier. To strike the cue ball exactly where I intend to appears to be the easiest thing in the game, but in fact it is the hardest. Most amateurs play screw shots by striking too high. Result: no backspin has been applied. The fear of 'jumping' the ball or cutting the cloth is the main reason for players not striking low enough. Then there is the player who goes too 'low' and continually 'jumps' or miscues the cue ball. The place to strike the cue ball safely is midway between the centre of the cue ball and 6 o'clock. If you improve your cueing and continually strike here for your stun or screw shots, then all that remains to stun to a stop or screw back from 1″ to 4 yards is the power and 'feel' we impart through the cue, and the cue tip, to the cue ball.

To play these shots correctly the bridge hand must be lowered. Do this by turning the bridge hand over until the body weight is on to the base of the thumb, and the tip of the little finger barely reaches the cloth. This, in effect, lowers the groove between thumb and forefinger in which the cue runs. The bridge hand grip is firm. Having lowered the tip to the cue ball by lowering the bridge hand, the next step is to lower the cue hand, so that the whole cue is down and horizontally level. Do not play downward strokes when addressing the bottom of the cue ball for screw shots – you have to play straight into the ball.

The action for stun-screw is shorter than the normal back stroke. The forward stroke is also shorter than normal, because of our 'shortened-up' stance. The distance of my follow through on a screw shot is 3″. On impact with the cue ball, I take a distinctly stronger hold on the cue without checking the action. This applies the 'bite'. It is the prolonged grip of the tip on the cue ball, plus the bite of the stroke itself, that creates the backspin.

Feel the screw as you apply it, from your cue hand, through the cue, to the tip onto and into the ball. Do not swing through the ball, but strike it with a crisp, clean stroke. The difference between screwing back 12″ and the length of the table is only the power put into the shot.

The two main obstacles against playing screw shots successfully are the distance between cue ball and object ball, and the thickness of contact when putting the pot down.

1. The further the balls are apart, the more power has to be applied to keep backspin on the cue ball till it reaches the object ball.
2. For the cue ball to be screwed back, contact of cue ball onto object ball has to be thick. Contact of less than half ball is not enough to get the cue ball anywhere but across the table after contact. I can alter the pull of the cue ball after thin contact on the object ball, but only slightly, by adding side to the screw. This, of course, makes the pot harder to get, and unless a player is advanced with his cueing, it is without doubt one of the hardest strokes to play in the game.

When attempting a screw shot, consider the distance between the cue ball and your 'target' ball, and look closely at the angle of your pot so that you know if contact will be thick enough to allow a screw back to be played.

To check over the main points for screw shots again:

(a) Make sure of the pot.
(b) Screw is reverse spin.
(c) A firm tip is ideal.
(d) Make sure of striking low.
(e) Stance to be firmer than normally.
(f) Lower the tip, and the butt, of the cue.
(g) The cue action is shorter, with a snappy, striking movement, tightening the grip on impact.

When first learning to screw back, make straight pots so that you are playing full onto the object ball with the cue ball. Commence your practice by playing with just enough power to pull the cue ball back several inches from a distance of 12″. Add power gradually until you can pull back several feet.

Remember, before you can hope to screw back the length of the table, you have to learn first to screw back half the length of the table, then by adding to the power of your stroke, screw back a little further each time till you can screw back twelve feet or more. It is very rarely that one wishes to screw the cue ball back any further than twelve feet.

## 32A, B – Stun (Straight Through)

With the cue ball and object ball being left in a similar position, this time the desired positioning of the cue ball was to travel forward only half the distance as the previous follow through because, in this instance, the black was further down the table. This shot is played with added power to the last shot (31A), again allowing the cue to go through. Striking point on the cue ball now, however, is 14. (Plate A shows shot before being played, Plate B shows result.)

32A
32B

## 33A, B – Stun (Angle Pot)

This shot is played with the same power as the stun through (32). Now, however, there is to be no follow through with the cue arm. I stop my cue on striking the cue ball by taking hold of the cue on impact. By closing my cue hand firmer on the cue at impact with the cue ball, it provides a 'deadener' on the cue ball. *Stop your cue arm on impact, as well*. Striking point on the cue ball – 15. (Plate A shows shot before being played, Plate B shows result.)

33A
33B

## 34 – Stun (Angle Across)

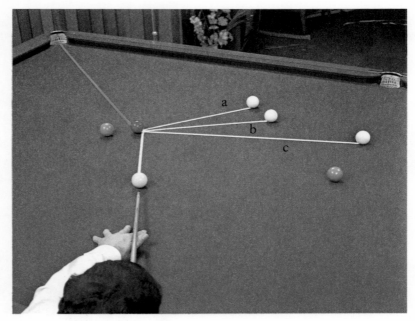

34

Shows an angle to the intended pot. Now because cue ball contact on to the object ball is approximately a half ball contact, I cannot expect to stun straight through, or hold, without sacrificing the pot by striking the object ball too full.

The pocketing of the object ball is first and foremost. The contact must be half ball. In playing position, however, there are several lines away to the right of the object ball that I can dictate the cue ball to follow.

The line will be determined by my striking point of cue tip on to cue ball, and the strength I put into the stroke.

I ask you to study this plate seeing:

1. The red line of the object ball to the intended pocket.
2. The white lines of the cue ball away on just three lines that could be used in gaining your desired position.

Striking point on the cue ball to follow: – line (a) would be 15; line (b) would be 6 o'clock; and line (c) would also be 6 o'clock. Note here the different direction acquired from line (b) to line (c) when both shots were played at 6 o'clock to the cue ball. The reason for the change of angle away from the red ball is also the reason for the extra travel of cue ball (c). The shot was played with added power. My intention on the first two shots (in the stun family) was to hold for the pink, the third shot my intention was to position on the blue for the centre pocket. I will deal with this technique more fully in Practice later on.

# 35 – Screw (Back)

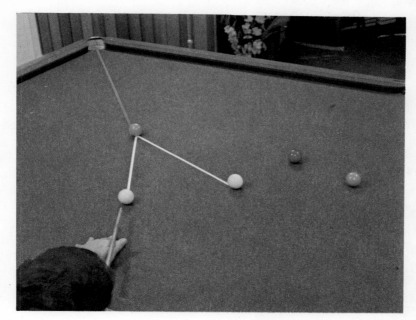

35

The required essentials here are to chalk your cue carefully; address the cue ball at 6 o'clock; take a firmer grip than normal with your bridge and cue hands; shorten your bridge to 8", at the same time shortening your gripping point with your cue hand to suit; play your stroke with a smooth, controlled, rhythmic drive, delivering your cue into and through the cue ball, with as much follow through as possible, without moving forward, off balance.

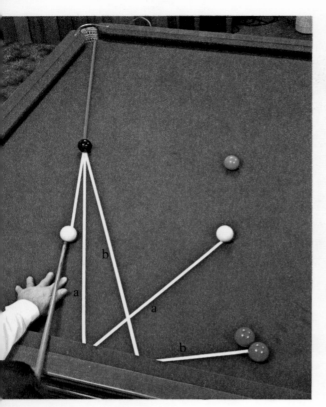

36

## 36 – Screw (Back with Side)

Here is a straight pot on the black. I intend not only to screw back to the side cushion in front of me, but to send the cue ball down the table to split the two reds.

To screw back without side, in potting the black, my cue ball would not reach the two reds (as indicated by white line (a), after striking the cue ball at 6 o'clock, and contacting the black full, ensuring the pot).

To move the cue ball further to my right, from the cushion in front of me, from white line (a) to white line (b), thus ensuring the splitting of the two reds, *side* has to be applied as well as backspin.

To move my cue ball to my right, after it comes back to the cushion from the black ball, the cue ball must be struck on the left. Low to bring it back from the black ball, left to make it pull to the right on reaching the cushion. Therefore, striking point on the cue ball, 7 o'clock.

In striking the cue ball at 7 o'clock, and at the desired speed to make sure the cue ball gets into the reds with enough power to split them open, allowance has to be made in your aiming onto the black ball. I will explain how and why in my next chapter on The Effects of Side, but in Plate 36 I ask you to note a second black ball placed against the cushion, and near to the intended corner pocket.

I have placed the second black ball there to indicate to you that I am aiming the cue ball at the black on its spot to the position the second black is occupying near the corner pocket. When I strike the cue ball at 7 o'clock and at the speed I intend to, I will make the black right into the pocket! You wonder why? The reason is that when I strike the cue ball low and left at 7 o'clock, the force of my cue going into the cue ball will force it away to the right of my intended aiming point on the black. This, in turn, will send the black not to the second black, but to the pocket. Just as well I allowed for this movement of the cue ball, in my aim!

## 37 – Screw (Deep)

To be played exactly as the screw back shown and explained in Plate 36. *Remember,* however, to increase the distance you intend to bring the cue ball back, by applying backspin, striking point on the cue ball must be 6 o'clock, and added power from the cue arm determines the distance of the cue ball travel.

37

## 38A, B – Screw (Black to Yellow)

Two shots often called for in top snooker, in gaining best position on yellow, before taking all the colours. Line (a) away from black, direct to the desired position, without touching a cushion will be achieved by striking cue ball at 5 o'clock. Line (b) using one cushion to the desired position will be achieved by striking cue ball at 7 o'clock with added power. Cue ball movement to black will have to be allowed for in aiming in both cases.

38A, B

49

# Side

The use of side can be a source of great satisfaction and accomplishment. However, I am bound to warn you that it could create trouble, so my advice to players in the early stages of learning to play snooker is *'don't use side'*.

When a player becomes good enough to control his cue action really well, then by all means let him use side, but only then when it is really necessary. Even then, use it when the cue ball has only a short distance to travel to the object ball. Using side on long shots is extremely dangerous. Some professionals, as well as amateurs of all grades, use side on the cue ball when it has to travel the length of the table before making its first contact. These shots are so uncertain that mostly, when they succeed, it is just through luck. The amount of allowance to be estimated, in making these side shots of push off and swerve back of the cue ball in playing soft, medium or power shots, is nothing more than a rough guess.

What does happen when we apply side? Most people think that when they hit the cue ball on the right side, it will immediately start curving away to the right! This is not the case. The first bite of the cue tip into the right side of the cue ball will push it out to the left until the initial impetus is spent and then the right hand side exerts itself and pulls the ball to the right. This, in fact, means that when the ball has side (spin) applied to it, a curve takes place which is subject to all sorts of fluctuations and degrees. The effect of side is created by the nap of cloth: the heavier the nap, the more spin effect.

Yet another factor is the speed at which the stroke is played: the more power that is applied when using side, the longer the travel of the cue ball will be before curving back after the push-off is exhausted.

If the distance between the cue ball and object ball is four feet, the cue ball, with right hand side applied, at less than medium pace, would have time to recover from being pushed out to the left and would move off its line to the right. Some allowance would therefore have to be made for this movement when sighting. Playing the same stroke with power would mean that the cue ball would hardly have recovered from its push-off to left, created by the impact of the cue tip to the right side of the ball, by the time it reached the object ball. Texture of the nap will affect these calculations, as will variations in the weather. Slackness of the cloth will affect the grip of a spinning ball. More especially, there is a difference when using side (spin) with and against the nap.

You will now appreciate the complications of using side. I use it only when positively necessary, and I hope to convince you also to play the game safely, as I do.

Previously I have written on the importance of stroking your cue on a horizontal plane, and when applying side to the cue ball, this is more important than for most shots.

When using side on the cue ball for a close shot, allowance must be made for the amount of 'push-off' when aiming. When the cue ball and the object ball are further apart, allowance for swing back must be made in aiming. The amount of 'push-off' and 'swing back' can only be regulated by the power of the stroke and by the amount of *side imparted*. If the side is weak, the cue tip strikes the cue ball just off centre, but if it is strong, it will strike the cue ball well out to the side.

To get an understanding of the amount of 'push-off' or 'swing back' when applying side, place the black ball on its spot and the cue ball 18″ from the black so that the pot is not straight, but there is a half ball contact to pot the black ball in the right hand pocket at the black spot end. This would make the black a straight pot to the top cushion, approximately 24″ back from the centre of the pocket. This now means that right hand side applied to the cue ball will be 'running' side and the left hand side will 'check' the cue ball.

For this test of 'push-off' we will use *right* side. Aim to pot the black, striking the cue ball midway between the centre of the ball and the right edge. Use sufficient power to make the cue ball travel to the top cushion and down to the centre pocket after black ball contact on a table of average speed. The cue ball will strike the side cushion approximately 6″ above the right centre pocket. However, if you have been aiming to pot the black ball into the middle of the top right hand pocket and have actually struck the cue ball midway between its centre and the right edge with enough power for the cue ball to reach the centre pocket, you will have missed by several inches to the right of the pocket on the side cushion. This is because you pushed the cue ball away from the cue tip to the left, overcutting the black ball when the cue ball travelled its 18″ to the black. Allowance should have been made for push off in aiming to pot the black when using the right hand side.

*Remember:* The more power used the greater the 'push-off'. A soft stroke will generate practically no 'push-off' at all.

Combining *side with screw* is often very useful, but it is certainly going to complicate the shot and add to the possibility of the shot going wrong.

Only a very good cueist can add side to a screw shot with any degree of consistent success. Cueing has to be confident, and positively first class. This is a shot where one has to have the knowledge of what will happen when:

(a) The cue tip strikes the cue ball, softly, moderately, or with drive.

(b) Side is used sparingly, moderately or excessively.

For a thorough understanding of what is going to happen when strokes combining side and screw are employed, when these strokes should be used, and how much side and screw to use, my advice to any learner (and for that matter, most experienced players) is to have a private lesson from a professional player, as there are many items to be understood which I cannot explain here because of limited space.

From the safety angle, the best way to use screw is the plain straightforward stroke, with a smooth follow through, using a very firm grip. Professional players vary in their methods of achieving a given amount of screw, depending on their touch, technique and skill. A learner's degree of application will also vary as he improves so that, when he can screw back 12″ when 15″ from the object ball and playing his stroke at a certain speed and hitting his cue ball at a certain depth, he will find that, as his timing and technique improve, the cue ball will come back a little further all the time.

Practise your cue shots this way: Place the balls 12″ apart and play a medium pace full ball screw back. Note the distance the cue ball comes back. Play continuously at that distance, steadily increasing the power until you have doubled and trebled the distance of screw back. Do not let your aim slip. Make certain you are potting your ball.

You must allow for the effect of the nap when making shots using side. The nap runs from the baulk end to the spot end of the table. There are thousands of threads from the baulk end to the spot (top) end, each made up of a mass of tiny fibres fitting into and overlapping each other like scales on a fish.

This nap affects all medium and slow strokes with and against the lay of the nap, but has very little effect across the nap.

In fast or power strokes, the pace of the stroke discounts nap effect. In slow or medium paced strokes, the nap, when applying side (spin), exercises strong influence. The effect of side up the table (with the nap) increases in proportion as the ball slows down.

With medium and slow strokes against the nap it will take effect in a contrary way. Instead of the cue ball spinning away to the right, when struck on the right side by the cue tip, it turns to the *left*. Across the table, the side and nap effect on straight shots is practically non-existent. In diagonal and slow shots, it does operate to some extent.

With and against the nap it is the pulling away tendency of the cue ball that we have to take into account, and as we know, the pull is in a different direction with the nap than against it.

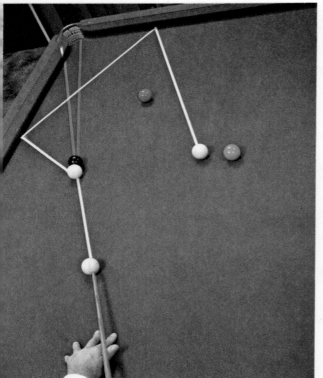

To run through the object ball and expect the cue ball on reaching a cushion to pull to the right, then the cue ball should be struck high on the right side (1 o'clock). To screw back and expect the cue ball to pull to the right after contact with a cushion, the cue ball should be hit low on the left side (7 o'clock) – the opposite to going forward.

## 39 –Side
## (Left, Run Through Black)

Here is a position often attained while playing snooker. I am nicely on the black ball and I intend to run through the black to the top cushion, side cushion, out around and nicely behind the red ball.

39

Red line indicates path of black to pocket. White line indicates intended path of the cue ball and the three cue balls show the stroke, point of contact and finishing position. Striking point of cue tip to cue ball will be 2 o'clock. (Some top to make cue ball run, combined with right spin to pull cue ball around the two cushions, on the intended line.)

A smooth follow through of the cue is essential. Let the cue follow through after impact onto the cue ball. Aim on to black ball has to allow for movement of the cue ball, on its journey to the black ball. The speed of stroke to be used in gaining desired position will determine the amount of 'push-off' of cue ball to black ball. In turn this governs the distance from pocket the black ball is to be aimed at to allow for that 'push-off'. White mark on cushion indicates position I will aim black to. After 'push-off' has taken place, correct contact onto the black ball as indicated by the second cue ball will result in the black following the intended line to pocket.

## 40 – Side (Check Against Running)

Shows exactly the same position on the black ball. The intention on this occasion is to firstly pot the black, and in doing so, to check the cue ball off the top cushion only, for desired position on the red ball. From this position check side will be left side – striking point on cue ball, 10 o'clock.

Smooth follow through is again essential, strength of stroke important, and applying opposite spin, as compared to last shot, means aiming allowance on to black ball will be opposite to spin previously used. Note white mark on cushion, adjacent to pocket, black ball is to be aimed at.

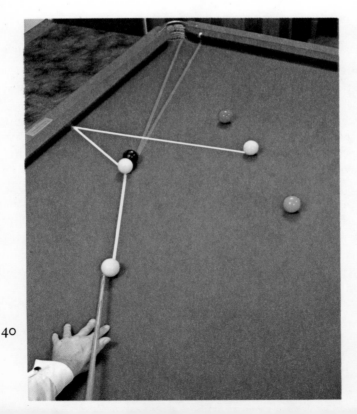

40

## 41 – Side (Soft Shot)

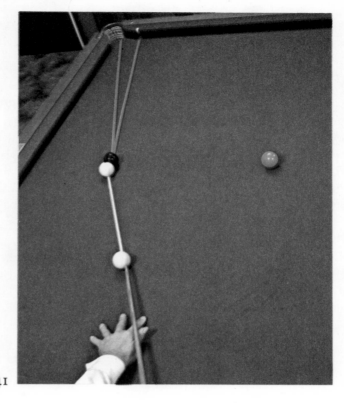

41

Both previous shots have had to be played with medium-paced strength, and allowance has had to be made for movement away from cue tip of cue ball. Plate 41 shows a shot set up where again side is to be applied to the cue ball. The strength now intended for positioning the cue ball is going to be soft.

Playing into the cue ball with right hand side, with a smooth follow through, at slow speed and with more of a push than a stroke, very little 'push-off' of cue ball from cue tip is going to take place. As the right spin (striking point on cue ball – 3 o'clock) is going to be strong, however, aim on to black ball will have to be the same as the last shot, but for a different reason. Now the spinning cue ball will affect the black object ball.

The applied right spin on a soft shot will 'throw' the object ball the opposite way – *left*, always, provided the cue ball is struck on the right with sufficient strength for spin still to be active on cue ball when it reaches black ball. On Plate 41 my aiming point on the black ball is to send it to the white mark on the far side pocket jaw (as indicated). The spin from the cue ball *(right)* will *not* transfer to the black ball – but will throw the black ball the opposite way – to the left – and thus into the pocket along correct path as indicated.

## 42 – Side (Power Shot)

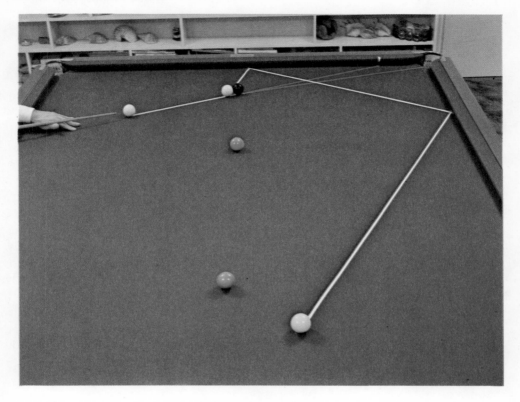

The same shot as the previous one, using the same intended side on the cue ball.

In this instance, however, the shot is to be played with power to force the cue ball around the angles and down the table. The striking point on the cue ball is going to be the same as shown and described in Plate 42. In this case, however, the black ball is aimed to the white mark shown on the opposite side of the pocket. Whereas on the soft shot (Plate 41) I had to allow for the spinning cue ball throwing the black object ball. In this case, because power is required, I must make allowance for the cue ball being pushed away from the cue tip. Cue ball and object ball will follow the paths as shown.

# Practice

To improve your snooker, you must practise. Then for your practice to be beneficial to you, it should be carried out regularly and along correct lines.

When about to practise, do not worry about finding an opponent. Playing with an opponent all the time may keep you in form, but practising along sound lines by yourself will bring more rapid improvement.

Two players setting about to play a frame of snooker together, especially when learning the game, do not realize how difficult they are making it for each other to improve their game. What usually happens is that the first player breaks the reds and only three or four come out, and he has the cue ball back in baulk. Unless one red has found its way over a pocket, his opponent has been left a reasonably hard shot to try and score. So both players have not much chance of scoring on their opening strokes. After several shots, one usually sees five reds still jammed together with the five or six remaining reds hard against the cushions. Not very good conditions for learning to pot or learning to position the cue ball. To make matters even worse, several colours may also be against the cushions, because following potted reds the colours have been missed and are off their spots. Nobody can go on potting hard balls.

A champion at snooker undoubtedly has the ability to work the cue ball around the table in making good position, thus making each following pot easy. This is the main reason for big breaks. In Australia today there are hundreds of good potters but there are few champions at snooker. The main reason, I consider, is that very few players practise correctly and sufficiently long enough to become proficient at sighting, cueing and touch. Then again, it is no good being a sound position player if you are missing your pots. We must learn to pot first.

## 43A – Practice (Plain White Only, Centre Spots)

Learn to groom accurate cueing:

(a)  Place cue ball on brown spot.
(b)  Aim to fire cue ball over pink spot.
(c)  Strike cue ball dead centre, 14.
(d)  Strike with sufficient power to return over brown spot.

If cue ball returns over brown spot, then cueing has been perfect. If cue ball returns to right or left of brown spot after passing over pink spot on way up table, the cueing has been bad. If cue ball pulls to right or left after striking top cushion, left or right hand side has been applied. Keep practising until cue ball travels up and down table over the spots, shot after shot.

## 43B – Practice (Plain White Only, Left and Right Baulk)

This exercise is to apply and control side (spin).

(a)  Place cue ball on brown spot.
(b)  Aim to fire cue ball over pink spot.
(c)  Strike cue ball 3 o'clock (to pull to right), 9 o'clock (to pull to left).
(d)  Strike with sufficient power to strike side cushions (where baulk line meets cushions).

Smooth, groomed cueing will ensure the cue ball will travel over pink spot on way to top cushion. Applied spin then pulling cue ball to where baulk line meets cushions. If cue ball is struck at 3 o'clock (pull to right) or 9 o'clock (pull to left) and does not pull out to fulfil ultimate aim, shot has probably not been played with enough power, therefore spin has gone from cue ball, by the time it has reached the top cushion.

## 43C – Practice (Plain White Only, Below Centre Pockets, Left and Right, Excessive Side)

This practice exercise is similar to Plate 43B. However, to pull cue ball acutely enough to reach side cushions above centre pockets, more power is essential. Apply added power to this shot, strike cue ball at 5 o'clock (pull to right) and 7 o'clock (pull to left) to achieve your object. Again true, groomed, fluent cueing is a must. Chalk tip well for these shots and keep cue as horizontally level as possible.

43A, B, C

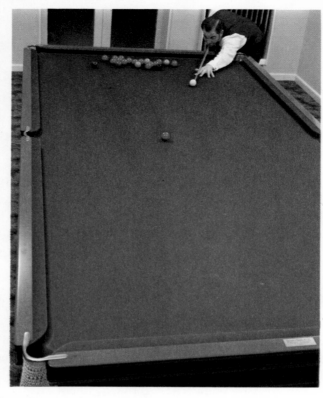

## 44 – Practice (Long Straight Pot)

A long, straight pot – probably my favourite practice technique for perfect cueing. Gather all 21 object balls into a corner of the baulk area of the table. Place one ball at a time halfway down the table (as shown), then position cue ball on the baulk line in a position setting the object ball up for a straight pot into the top corner pocket. You are setting out to pot all 21 object balls, one at a time, in this exercise. Vary the position of the object ball between the blue spot and the centre pockets so that you get an opportunity of playing the cue ball fully across the baulk line. You only need to play from off the baulk line the width of the 'D'.

To continually pocket this long, straight pot, your stance, aim and cueing will have to be perfect as you will not make the shot if any of those three vital fundamentals are not working correctly. On setting your stance and aligning your cue to play full on to the red ball, do not sight at the pocket, as you can see the pocket in the background. Your sighting concentration, at the time of delivering the stroke, should be on the red.

Strike the cue ball at point 15 intending to stun the cue ball at position where cue ball contacts object ball. Weight forward on to bridge arm and bridge hand. Rear leg remains straight, left knee bent with slightly more weight on the left foot than the right. A smooth, well groomed and fluent stroke is essential. Strike with a brisk action to stun the cue ball dead on contacting the object ball. Try to practise this type of shot for one hour each day.

45A

## 45A – Practice (Blue Only, Various Positions)

*Blue to pink from below left:* In practising this shot, which often occurs in snooker, the cue ball, in following the intended line, must have left spin applied checking cue ball against running on to side cushion. Aiming point on to blue is on the 'thickish' side to send blue to white mark indicated on the pocket jaw. The cue ball at address is to be struck at 10 o'clock. Left hand spin being applied to the cue ball will throw the blue to the centre of the pocket. Correct strength of stroke is essential. Ideal position on pink is achieved by use of only one cushion (top cushion) as shown.

## 45B – Practice (Blue Only, Various Positions)

*Blue to pink from below left:* From this position, centre ball striking (12 o'clock) on the cue ball allows sighting on to blue to centre of middle pocket (no spin effect). Desired path of cue ball from this natural angle will be off two cushions for ideal position.

45B

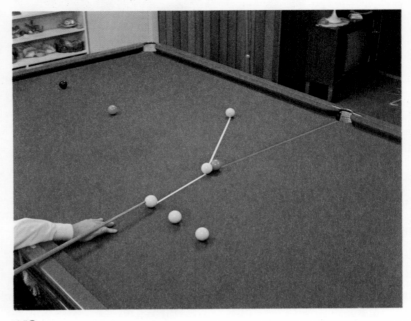

45C

## 45C – Practice (Blue Only, Various Positions)

*Blue to pink from below left:* Again 12 o'clock striking of the cue ball on to blue (aimed to centre of middle pocket) will result in the cue ball following a shorter, direct path to same desired position.

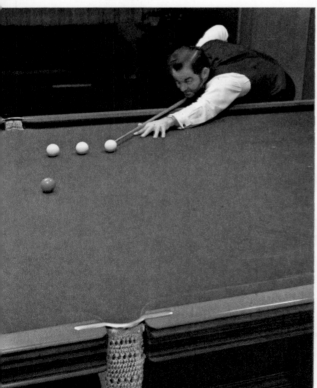

## 45D, E, F – Practice (Blue Only, Various Positions)

*Blue to pink below right:* These three shots from similar positions on the opposite side of the table are to be played the same way, except that on Plate 45A striking point now is 2 o'clock instead of 10 o'clock.

45D, E, F

## 46A – Practice (Pink Only, From Bottom Left to Corner Pocket)

From nearest cue ball, aim to pocket pink ball to the centre of the pocket with sufficient power to position cue ball along indicated path. Striking point on the cue ball, 15. Clip the cue ball cleanly with a brisk stroke.

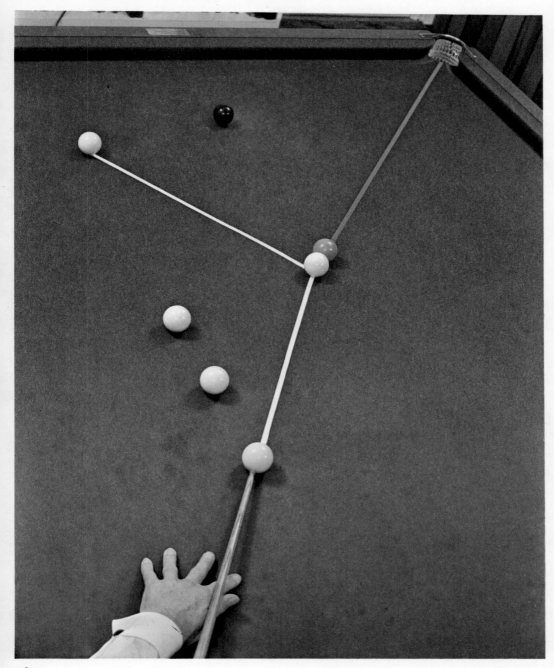

46A

## 46B – Practice (Pink Only, From Bottom Left to Corner Pocket)

From second cue ball (off straight), aim pink ball to centre of pocket. Striking point on cue ball, 12 o'clock. Play with sufficient strength for cue ball to travel indicated path to side cushion and off to point shown.

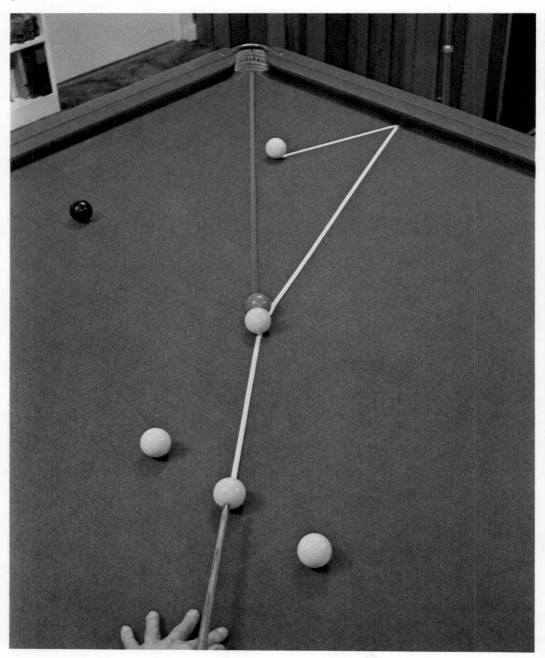

46B

# 46C – Practice (Pink Only, From Bottom Left to Corner Pocket)

From third cue ball, aim to overcut pink to white mark on top cushion. Strike cue ball at 5 o'clock with power for cue ball to follow intended path to Point C. The drive of the cue tip at 5 o'clock on the cue ball will automatically push cue ball thicker into pink ball than aim intended, because of the power used, taking pink ball cleanly into pocket.

46C

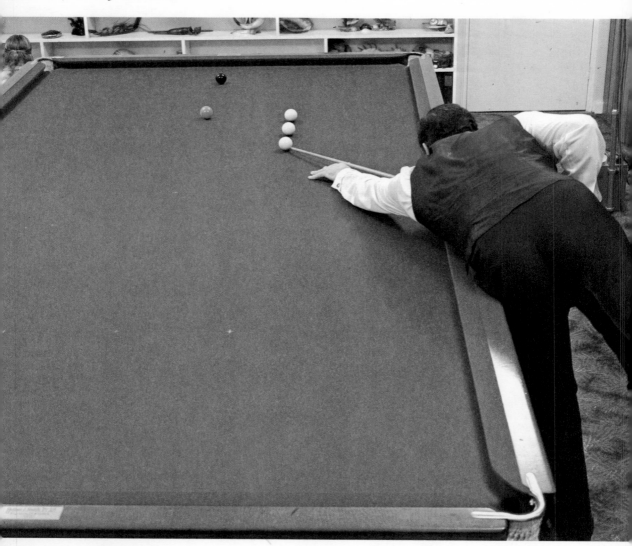

46D, E, F

## 47A – Practice (Pink Only, From Above Left to Middle Pocket)

From cue ball, aim pink ball to centre of middle pocket along intended path shown. Strike cue ball at 12 o'clock with a smooth follow through action that will allow the cue ball to travel the intended path. Some power is required for this shot.

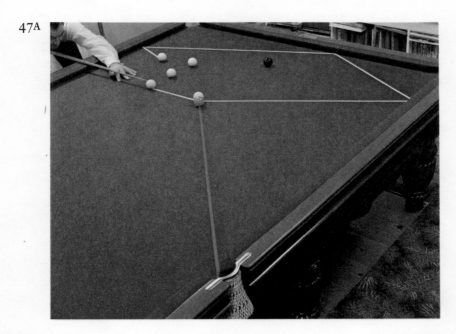

47A

## 47B – Practice (Pink Only, From Above Left to Middle Pocket)

From cue ball aim pink ball to centre of middle pocket, striking cue ball below centre at 15. This is a stun shot to force cue ball to travel intended path to point for position on black ball at opposite side of table. To apply stun effect to the cue ball (*no* follow through of the cue ball), stop the cue on striking cue ball.

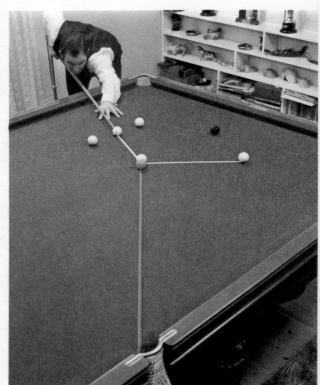

47B

## 47C – **Practice (Pink Only, From Above Left to Middle Pocket)**

From cue ball (near straight pot position), aim pink ball to centre of middle pocket. Strike cue ball at 6 o'clock. Screw back on same line from pink ball back to ideal position on black ball.

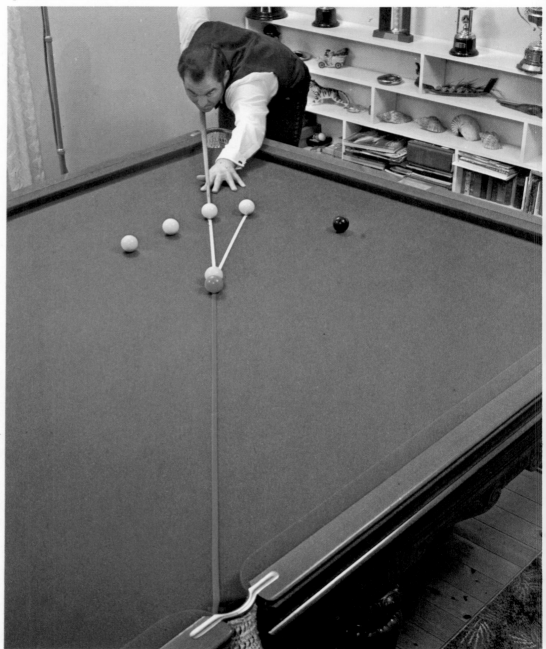

## 47D, E, F –Practice
### (Pink Only, From Above Right to Middle Pocket)

These three shots from similar positions on the opposite side of the table are to be played the same way.

All these shots in the 47 group are ones I consistently play, because on each occasion I can get from pink ball to black ball without applying side spin on any of the six shots employed. I have continued to strike with vertical centre striking on the cue ball, as I advocate for most pot shots in the game.

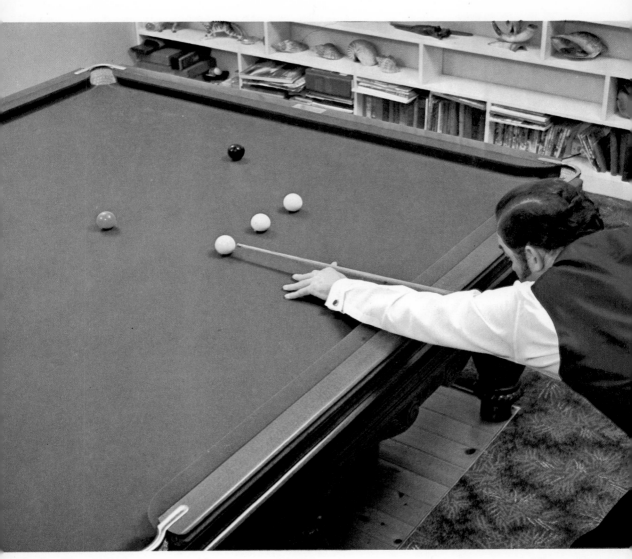

47D, E, F

## 48A, B, C, D — **Practice (Pot Black 200 Times)**

Over the years I have spent many hours on this special practice technique of potting the black off its spot from the position shown 200 times. The position of the cue ball is not the position to keep coming back to, it is merely the commencing position. The exercise combines positional play with potting. Therefore, after each pot, you should be leaving yourself in the desired position for your next shot.

The four shots indicated on Plate 48 are four shots that can be played in the following order and are just four of my favourite ways of keeping the cue ball back on to the black:

1. Plate 48A. Aim black ball to centre of the pocket shown by red line. Cue ball to follow path of line to point shown. Striking point on cue ball 12 o'clock. Correct strength of stroke is very important.
2. Plate 48B. Aim black to centre of the pocket. Striking point on cue ball 13, for intended travel of cue ball to point shown. Strength of stroke again important.

48A

48B

3.  Plate 48c. Aim black to centre of the pocket. Striking point on cue ball 15, with sufficient strength for cue ball to follow intended path to point shown.
4.  Plate 48d. Aim black to centre of the pocket. Striking point of cue ball 12 o'clock, again with sufficient strength for the cue ball to follow intended path travelling two cushions to point shown.

These are four potting and positional shots, played in sequence on the black, always aiming the cue ball on to the black to centre of corner pocket without any side spin (left or right) ever being applied to cue ball. If you repeat these moves, along with quite a few other positioning shots, you are well on the way to potting the black ball the 200 intended times. What better practice than this for becoming proficient at potting the black from off its spot?

48c

48d

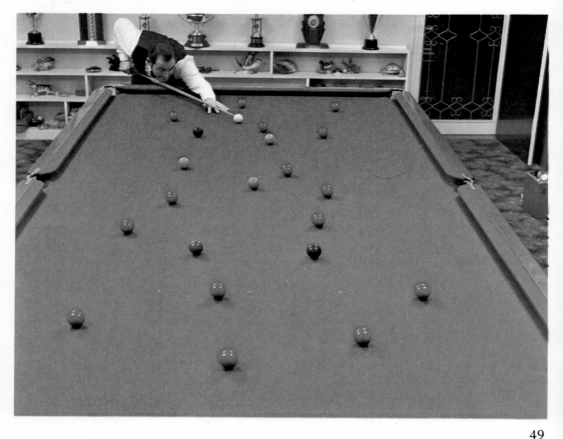

49

Place the 21 object balls, spread out, all over the table. Keep them out from the cushions and apart, keeping in mind that this is to be straight-out potting. Do not worry about getting a red then a colour. Pot anything. The idea is that because there are six pockets on the table and 21 balls to be potted, you are getting a pot at each pocket, and practically every shot you play will be a different angle.

You set yourself the task of trying to pot the 21 shots. When you can do this, you have become proficient at the first stage of snooker. You are learning to pot as the champions do. If at first you find that you have taken, say, 40 or 50 shots to put the lot down, count your misses, set them up again and try to beat your last score. You will see that when you make your first pot there are several reds to choose from, but as you thin them out, you have also to pay more attention to positional play. In practising this 21 ball technique from the start, play reasonable position by at least concentrating on keeping the cue ball out from cushions. You should never finish with the cue ball against a cushion. Place the cue ball anywhere to start, keep concentrating, and keep at it.

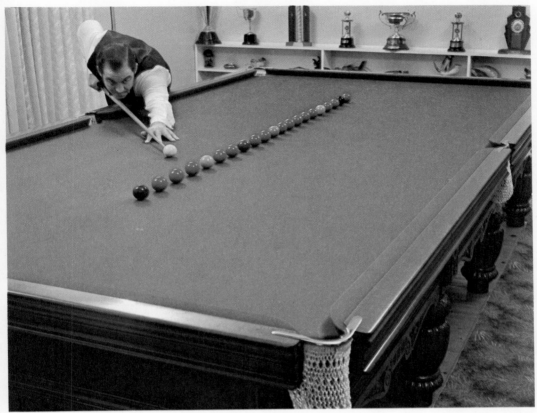

50

This is a practice technique that I have used since my early playing days on advice I received as a schoolboy from the late and great Walter Lindrum. It is marvellous practice for learning the potting angle and adding cue ball control at the same time.

The task I set myself here, and advise you to adopt, is to line all 21 object balls down the centre of the table; you should fit them between the brown and pink spots. Use your cue to pull them into a reasonably good line, and put cue ball into a handy position to start. The task you are setting yourself all the time is to take all 21 object balls, without a miss, and to do so without the cue ball ever touching the cushions.

Again we apply the three important points I have previously outlined to you:

1. The potting of the object ball.
2. The correct striking of cue tip on to cue ball.
3. The feel of your cue, as to how hard or how soft to play each shot for a gaining position.

Place the cue ball into a handy position to start, making an angle to the first pot.

First and foremost, all the time, pocket the object ball. This is plain, straight out good sighting judgement backed up, of course, with a good cue action.

Positioning the cue ball around the table is a combination of two things:

(a) Where you strike the cue ball with the tip of your cue which will dictate to the cue ball the angle you want it to come away from the object ball on; and

(b) The strength of the stroke, which will further determine how far the cue ball is going to travel along the intended line.

In setting out to take all 21 object balls without a miss and without the cue ball ever touching the cushion, I have to look ahead. I unfailingly pocket all 21 object balls without a miss, time after time. Yet when I set out to clear the balls again, I never set out looking 21 shots ahead, as I have no set technique in taking the 21 object balls; I will, however, look ahead at least as far as this shot and the next: what am I going to pocket now, what area am I going to move the cue ball into, and what is my next shot going to be?

To regularly and consistently carry out this exercise, I make an angle on my next shot each time. It is the angle that I make on each object ball that enables me to work up and down the line without ever touching the cushions. If I make a straight pot, I can only run through that pot to the other side of the table or I can only draw back. When commencing this practice technique, however, you will soon find out that you cannot work from the extreme ends of the balls if you are making straight pots. You must create an angle to your pots to be able to carry out the exercises and I make an angle that allows me to pull the cue ball away from the line of balls and not risk the problem of having my cue ball kissing, and getting caught up in, the line of balls.

In practising this marvellous technique for potting, positioning and developing touch, do not run the cue ball through or draw it back too far, leaving too much distance between the line of balls or running the risk of getting the cue ball back near a cushion. At the same time, do not under-hit your shots leaving the cue ball too close into the balls as, from a position like that, you will find that there are no balls on because you could not play them past one another, for the corner pockets in particular. Concentrate on keeping the cue ball a comfortable distance from the line of balls and no further back than say, halfway between the line of balls and the side cushion.

## 51 – Practice (Advance Line Up)

Now you see the colours on their correct spots. The line of reds are spaced in as follows: 1 above the black ball, 5 between black and pink balls, 7 between pink and blue balls, and 2 below the blue ball. We are now moving into the break building family of practice techniques.

Always set out from the position shown to make a 100 break or clear the table.

After each red, you must take a colour, after a colour back to the next red. I have passed 1,300 century breaks at snooker to this stage of my career. This is one of the practice techniques that has meant so much to me in acquiring my break building skill in matches at snooker. I have practised this advanced line up for hours and hours and hours during my career, always striving for accuracy in my potting and cue ball control by correct striking on to the areas of the cue ball called for in the 36 shots that I will have to play if I am to clear the table. I am working always to perfect my strength of stroke, for each and every shot will at times call for soft, medium and power strokes.

Again I have no set technique on how I will take the balls. I run the cue ball around cushions, across the table, down the table and up the table in my relentless pursuit of at least 100 break. I always count my break as it builds up, as I find this helps my concentration immensely, particularly in my big matches. When playing before an audience of 2,000 people, compiling a big break when I am concentrating correctly is little different, in fact, to compiling a big break in my own billiard room on my own, practising.

Try to keep clear of cushions. Do not get too close to the line of balls – always work to keep your cue ball clear of the line of balls. I realize that you would never see a situation in a game of snooker where the balls would come out as they are positioned now, however I have purposely placed the balls where they are so all the balls can be taken, providing my potting and positional play is good. This technique is tremendous for acquiring the skill that is needed to make big breaks in actual games at Club level, or even in Championship matches.

51

52

A second break building situation that I often use continually to perfect my break building technique. Again, as in Plate 51, set off by taking a red, a colour, a red, a colour, etc., always striving to clear the table or make a 100 break at least. Dedication with this type of practice will increase your potting ability and knowledge of positional play. Keep working hard at this technique and improvement is sure to come.

## 53A –Practice (Colours from Spots)

The picture shows the ideal position of cue ball to commence taking all six colours. Aim yellow ball to the centre of the pocket. Strike cue ball dead centre at 14. The desired strength is for cue ball to follow indicated path, finishing nicely on green.

## 53B –Practice (Colours from Spots)

Aim green to centre of pocket. Strike cue ball at 6 o'clock drawing cue ball directly off green to several inches outside of baulk line along intended path, to point shown. On striking cue ball, stop delivery of cue as for stun shot.

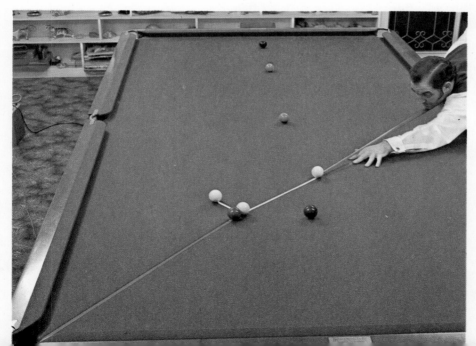

## 53C –Practice (Colours from Spots)

Aim brown ball to centre of pocket. Strike cue ball, below centre at 15 to follow intended path to side cushion and off to a point for perfect position on blue ball. This shot definitely has to be played at the right speed as finishing short will leave a difficult shot on the blue in attaining ideal position on the pink ball. The same will apply if the shot from brown ball is over-hit, resulting in cue ball travelling beyond the desired point. No side is required for this shot. The angle on cue ball to brown ball in making the pot is a natural angle when cue ball struck at 15.

53C

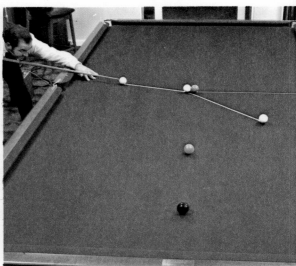

53D

## 53D –Practice (Colours from Spots)

Aim blue to centre of pocket. Striking point on cue ball, above centre at 13. A soft, smooth stroke will result in the cue ball following intended path from blue to a point shown for a near straight pink ball.

## 53E –Practice (Colours from Spots)

Aim pink ball to centre of pocket. Striking point on cue ball, above centre at 12 o'clock. A smooth follow through with your cue action with the right strength of stroke to follow through pink ball for good position on black ball.

53E                                    53F

## 53F –Practice (Colours from Spots)

Pot Black! Aim black ball to centre of the pocket. Strike cue .ball below centre at 15 stunning cue ball to a dead stop at point of contact, as shown. Remain steady and cue carefully in making certain of potting the black. Irrespective of how easy it looks this should get the full concentration that every shot in snooker deserves. I have seen this simple looking shot missed on many occasions by top players, as well as learners, simply because the shot is taken for granted.

This series of shots (53A to F) was a perfect way of clearing the table by taking all 6 colours. Having played a good shot by getting the cue ball into the desired opening position on the yellow, it is not difficult to take the remaining five coloureds, providing you do not shun your practice. I would hope that you have noticed that, by playing snooker the Eddie Charlton way, never once has your cue tip been away from the vertical centre line of the cue ball. That has to be good snooker!

# Doubling

An experienced player often recognizes that a scoring stroke can be made from a ball tucked up on a cushion, a stroke that would go unnoticed by an inexperienced player. The experienced player realizes that a ball can be doubled on to cushions, and around angles, in making scoring strokes.

On doubling, my technique in attempting a scoring shot, is to use only one cushion in preference to two, two cushions in preference to three, three cushions in preference to four, and so on, and never with excessive power.

Doubling is difficult even to the most experienced players. I attempt doubles always at a speed that will bring the object ball away from the intended pocket area, should I miss. In effect I attempt doubling on the basis that it is a shot to nothing, as I will have reasonable safety should I miss the shot. Any player attempting doubles has the odds against him, therefore I always consider the situation carefully before attempting the double, in case a safety shot may be in my better interests.

However there are occasions when a game can be won by doubling a ball by use of the cushions. I rarely double without the distinct possibility of being able to play a sound position shot to carry on with. In attempting doubles, do not play with any more power than you think is necessary, as a very common fault by most players is to force the object ball into a cushion at excessive speed. What invariably happens is that the ball, having been buried into the rubber cushion with no side applied to it in going on to the cushion, will have spin applied to it when it comes off. Having been thrown off the rubber cushion at speed and depending at which angle, that spin will react from the next cushion that it goes to, should more than one cushion be attempted. Most snooker players can never understand, when attempting a double across the table to a middle pocket, why the ball off the second cushion will straighten up and then spend the rest of its journey travelling backwards and forwards across the table instead of taking the angle the player was looking for.

Probably the main problem with doubling is finding the correct angle to the pocket. Try and keep in mind that a ball at slow to medium pace speeds with no spin applied to it, will come off a cushion on the same line of angle that it went on. Therefore, in assessing the line of the object ball to the pocket, you should be looking for the line of the red on to the cushion and from that point of the cushion to the pocket.

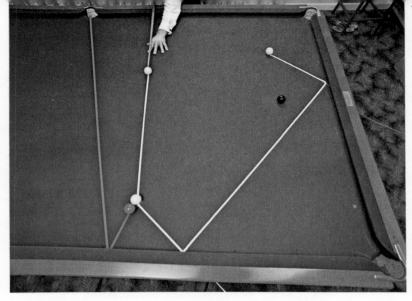

## 54A –Doubling (Single Ball, Off One Side Cushion)

Sight the line of the red ball to the cushion, allowing for it to come off the cushion on the same line to the intended pocket. Strike the cue ball at 13 to pass around the black ball, on intended line, for the black ball next shot. The strength that you have played the shot in acquiring cue ball to the indicated position is of sufficient strength for red ball to be clear of the intended middle pocket at that speed.

## 54B –Doubling (Single Ball, Off One Side Cushion)

We see a red ball close to the middle pocket but not on for that centre pocket for a direct shot because of the narrow opening at that angle. Cue ball is now into the desired position for making one of the simple doubles back into the middle pocket. The doubling of this particular red is easier to gauge than the last double because the line of the red to the cushion is going to be straighter for the red ball returning to indicated pocket. Strike cue ball at sufficient speed for position on black ball by striking cue ball at 8 o'clock when cue ball will follow desired path as shown.

54B

79

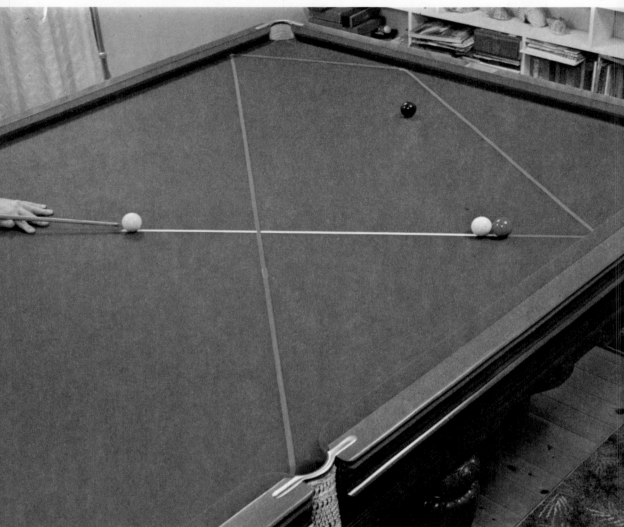

The red ball is in a position for a Marker's double. By this I mean sending the red ball straight ahead to the side cushion, top cushion, side cushion and middle pocket. Position on the black ball is assured and if the red ball is missed, there is a strong possibility of reasonable safety being obtained. The cutting of the red ball into the corner pocket is a distinctly risky shot, as the ball may be left in the jaws if under, or over, cut. I prefer the Marker's double and use it quite often. It is not a difficult shot to play when I have gained a knowledge of angles of the table I am playing on. Striking point on cue ball is 15, stunning the cue ball to a stop on contact position shown for ideal position on the black ball.

# Plant Shots

There are various types of plant shots that occur in snooker. Firstly there is the plant shot with balls touching that are not on to a pocket, but can be made on by pocketing the front ball, having struck the back ball on its correct contact point.

Secondly there is the plant shot where a back ball can be made 'in-off' the front ball. In making the far ball in the plant position shown in Plate 55A, the secret is the correct contact of the cue ball on to the right area of the nearest object ball. From the line of the two object balls to the jaw of the middle pocket it would appear that the front object ball would have to be struck on the right hand side (the obvious looking side). The contact point, however, is on the opposite side. Striking the nearest object ball on the left will squeeze that ball off to the right, and that near object ball will, in turn, carry the further object ball off to the right itself when the cue ball goes off to the left. With practice you can learn to contact on to the nearest red ball with the right contact (thin or thick depending on how much you intend to deflect the far object ball). In playing this shot, cue ball can be struck anywhere around its circumference, and at any speed.

## 55A – Plant Shots (Balls Touching – Front Ball)

Here you see me playing the shot three quarters full on to the left side of the first object ball deflecting the second object ball from off the plant line as indicated by the white mark on the cushion jaw to centre of pocket.

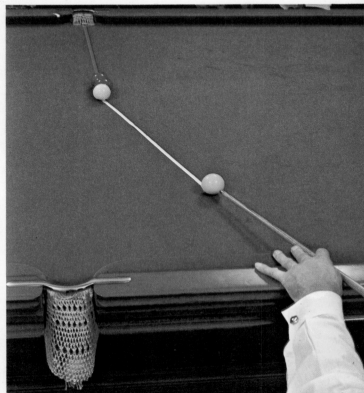

55A

## 55B – **Plant Shots (Balls Apart – Front Ball)**

A similar position to Plate 55A with the two balls planted on the same side of the jaw to the pocket opening; the difference this time is that the balls are apart. The far ball can again be made into the middle pocket but, because the balls are apart, on this occasion, the cue ball must be aimed to the right side of the nearest ball, so that the nearest ball goes off on line contacting the far ball on the correct point of contact, sending the far ball off on line to the pocket.

My technique for this particular shot is to sight the near object ball as a *cue* ball on to the far object ball in establishing the far object ball's line to the pocket. I then sight the area on the cushion in the background that the near object ball has to take, in striking the far object ball, to send it off on line to the pocket, and I simply get back behind the cue ball and aim the second object ball to the area I have picked out on the cushion. Be sure to play the shot with sufficient speed for the far object ball to reach the pocket.

Note the intended path of the cue ball on to the first object ball and the intended path of the first object ball on to the second object ball as marked in white. The contact point of the first object ball will send the second object ball along its intended path shown in red. The line of the first object ball on to the second object ball is taken to a point on the side cushion marked with a white mark. My sighting technique is to aim the first red ball from the angle to the cue ball in position shown to the white marker on the side cushion.

55B

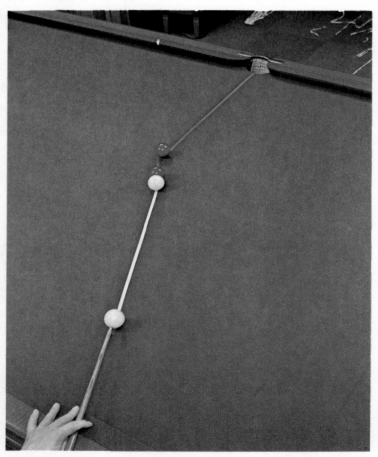

## 55C – Plant Shots (Balls Touching – Back Ball)

A situation where I have established that the line of the two object balls and the intended centre pocket are at right angles. I now realize that the back ball in this particular plant (touching or to within ⅛th inch apart) cannot be missed into the intended centre pocket. To send it off to the right, contact point is on the left – thick or thin. Again the shot can be made by striking the cue ball anywhere around its circumference, and at any speed. The shot cannot be missed as the back ball can only 'break-away' square.

55C

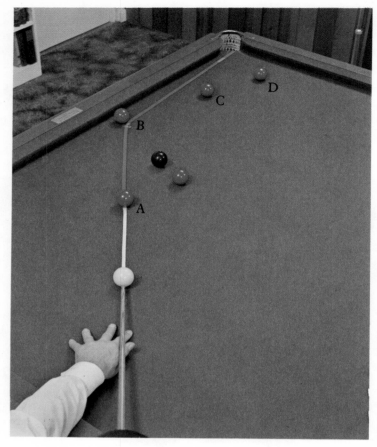

55D

## 55D – Plant Shots (Balls Apart – Back Balls, Red and Black)

The picture shows a position of five reds adjacent to the black ball. You are looking at the shot from behind the cue ball as I see it. There does not appear to be a ball on, but this is one of the occasions when a big break can commence by seeing an angle where one red ball can be played 'in-off' another red ball to commence the break. From the position left me when I approached the table, I could see that red A could be played 'in-off' red B to the corner pocket. It was also obvious if I stunned the cue ball to a stop on red A, that red C would block my ideal position on the black for the same corner pocket. On closer examination, however, I could also see by stunning the cue ball to a dead stop on red A, that I could continue the break by making the black ball 'in-off' red ball D, thus opening the way for what could be a substantial break.

In the first of the two shots required in making red A and then the black ball as described, I aim red ball A half a ball on to red B to take intended path as shown to pocket. Striking point on cue ball – 15 with a softish stroke to give red A every chance of getting into the closed, corner pocket at that angle.

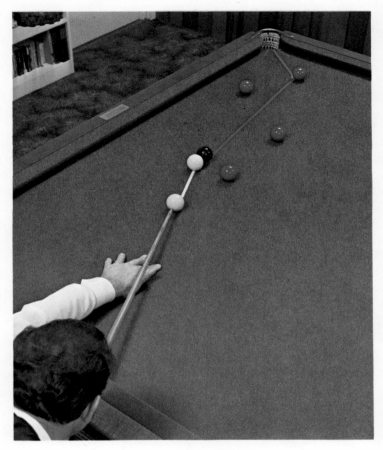

# 55E – Plant Shots (Balls Apart – Back Balls, Red and Black)

Following on from Plate 55D, in taking the black ball, I use a similar technique of sending the black ball straight ahead for half ball contact on to the red ball for 'in-off' into the corner pocket. Striking point on cue ball in potting black is 14, and a firm stroke is required to send black firmly on to red ball and into corner pocket. Ideal position on to the red ball covering the path of the black ball to the pocket will be achieved.

# Snookering

Laying snookers is a very important part of the game. Snookers can be played in the early part of a frame to get your opponent on the defensive and into trouble by forcing him to go off a cushion or around two or more cushions to hit the ball on (as there may still be 12 or 13 reds left at that stage). It is quite possible that your opponent will safely negotiate the snooker by hitting a red or reds that are on, which will give you the opportunity to commence what could be a frame winning break. Usually, however, snookers are employed later in a frame when a player needs the advantage of getting his opponent into trouble by laying a snooker with perhaps only one red left on the table, again looking for a leave should his opponent hit or even miss, the ball on. With the Foul Snooker and Play Again Rules that are now in the game of snooker, it is quite possible to get an advantage over your opponent with a snooker at that stage.

In the main, however, snookers are played for when there are not sufficient points left on the table towards the end of a frame for a player to win. The player now is forced to lay snookers in gaining the points allowed should his opponent fail to strike the ball on, from any such snooker laid. In attempting to lay snookers try to find an angle that you can play so that, besides your opponent being snookered on the ball on, distance between ball on and the cue ball has to be considered as well, adding to your opponent's worries and testing his knowledge of angles to the full.

## 56A – Snookering (Colours on Spot, One Red, Baulk End)

The last red ball is towards the bottom end of the table. I require a snooker to win. My intention here is to play thin to the outside edge of the red, cutting the red on to the first side cushion, and across to the opposite side cushion, and in behind the baulk colours along intended path shown. Cue ball to travel to bottom cushion on to side cushion and back down to finish with the black or the pink covering the red and putting distance between the cue ball and object ball. There is a possibility that other balls may finish between cue ball and the red ball as well. Striking point on the cue ball for this shot is 10 o'clock. Correct strength of stroke is extremely important here so that red ball travels the two intended cushions and back near the centre of the table, away from either corner pocket, with the cue ball at the top of the table, above the black ball.

# 56B – Snookering (Colours on Spot – One Red, Spot End)

The last red is at the opposite, top, end of the table with cue ball in position as shown. Requiring a snooker from this position I have the same thoughts again of not only acquiring a snooker but putting distance between cue ball and object ball, thus making the shot doubly difficult for my opponent. The way I would play this particular shot would be to aim full at the red ball striking the cue ball at 15 with sufficient strength to drive the object ball around two cushions along intended path shown, checking the cue ball in behind the black ball.

From this position I seldom play the cue ball from the red ball to the side cushion in behind the black ball, at the same time driving the red ball on to the top cushion back down the table, as at this angle it is very easy to misjudge the shot and have the cue ball return off the side cushion, meeting up and making contact with the red returning from the top cushion. Nine times out of ten, when this happens, the red ball is left on.

56B

## 56C – Snookering (Blue, Pink, Black)

A situation of blue, pink and black balls being left and a snooker required. A safe shot to try here, requiring a snooker to win, is to play thin to the left edge of the blue ball, cutting the blue over to the centre of the baulk cushion at sufficient speed for the cue ball to travel to top cushion, then side cushion, in an endeavour to get behind the black or pink balls. It is the type of shot I often look for as, in failing to gain the pink, I at least have acquired a reasonable safety shot. Striking point on the cue ball in sending the blue ball along the desired path, and the cue ball around its intended journey, is dead centre, 14.

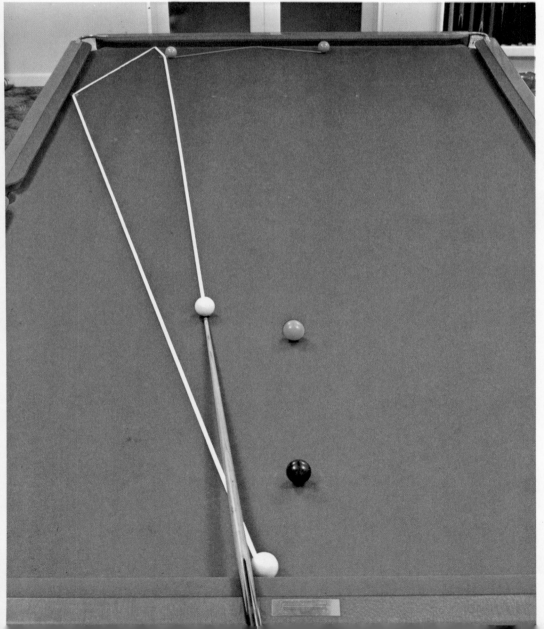

# Out of Snookers

Being forced to play out of snookers successfully, requires a similar knowledge to laying snookers and playing safety shots, i.e. a good knowledge of natural angles on a billiard table. There are very few snookers that could not be played out of, with a good knowledge of those angles.

It is not always getting out of the snooker that can be the problem, particularly with the class of player that I am continually opposed to, but hitting the object ball and getting it safe after successfully negotiating the snooker.

With these thoughts in mind, I may consider playing around angles with a dead strength shot, that would leave the cue ball as close to the object ball as possible so that after I have hit the ball on, or perhaps unluckily missed it, my opponent will have no chance of pocketing that ball.

Then again I may purposely play to get out of the shot by power, driving the object ball as far away from the cue ball as is possible after negotiating the snooker. My intention here would be to have as much distance between the balls as possible making it difficult for my opponent to score from the position left him. Whichever way I decide to play the shot, I will look for a way that is as foolproof as possible by using one cushion where I can in preference to two, or two cushions where I can in preference to three, and so on. I often employ the swerve shot to swing around the offending ball in getting out of a snooker, or apply the quicker turn by using a massé shot. It depends *so much* on the state of the game, and the number of points left on the table when I am confronted with these situations.

57A

Plate 57A shows a shot I recently had to play when snookered on the blue in behind the pink, as shown, with the black covering one side of the blue as well. I successfully negotiated the snooker off seven cushions as shown, and was quite confident of doing so before I played the shot, because of my knowledge of angles in the first instance, and the beautiful Heiron & Smith table I was playing on, in the second instance. Striking point on the cue ball for this shot 4 o'clock, with a very powerful stroke required to travel the seven cushions.

## 57B – Out of Snookers

Another way of getting out of a seemingly impossible snooker. There are usually several ways of getting out of snookers because of the various angles that can be taken on a billiard table. The shot that I preferred to play in this instance recently was to play on to the jaw of the top cushion, deflecting back on to the opposite jaw of the side cushion, cue ball finally travelling along the face of the top cushion as shown, to make contact with the blue ball. Striking point on the cue ball for this shot, 15. A firm stroke required so that backspin applied to the cue ball will remain on the cue ball on its journey to the first cushion, thus assisting the cue ball to stay down on the table, and not jump in the jaws, as so often can happen on billiard tables.

## 57C – Out of Snookers

An extremely nasty situation, where a medium-paced shot with strong left hand side resulted in my cue ball, travelling the indicated path to top cushion, returning to the bottom cushion, and on to the blue ball. Striking point on the cue ball, 10 o'clock. Correct speed of stroke for this particular shot is of paramount importance so that the cue ball will have the intended amount of spin applied to it when it hits the first cushion (top cushion).

57C

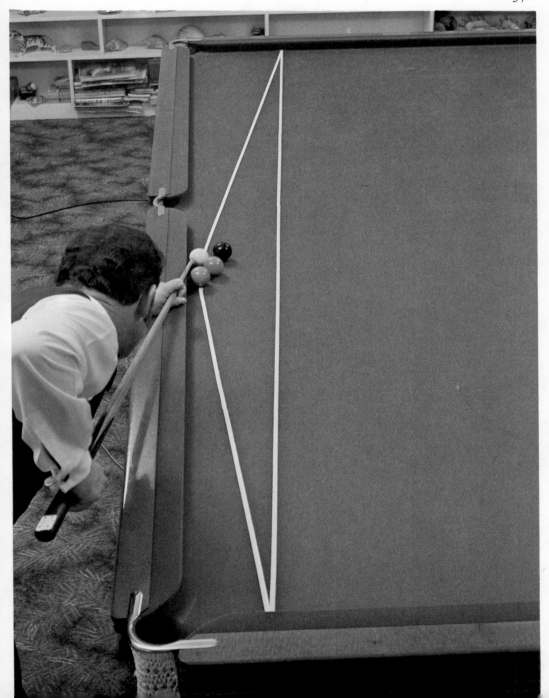

# Safety Play

Safety play I consider is a very technical, but important part of snooker play, particularly as played by professionals in the top bracket of snooker. The standard of snooker today among the top flight professionals, particularly in matches between Ray Reardon and myself, is that frame after frame can be won or lost depending on who gets the first red ball. The first player on so many occasions, will win the frame.

In striving to get in first, strong safety play can be a great ally. It can be the means of getting in first, for slowing your opponent down if the match is slipping away from you, and can be a strong tactical move halfway through a frame, or at the very end of a frame.

I look at successful snooker in three ways. Good, long, consistent potting, strong, reliable and consistent break building, and strong, determined safety play. I have won ever so many frames over my years as a professional player, through strong safety play in the first instance, the creation of the slightest opening when a good pot has got me in and the further result of a good break that has clinched the frame. They are tactics that have worked for me and helped one of my main ambitions to be the outstanding tournament winner in the game. Today I hold that distinction, having won more tournaments than any other living snooker player.

I will continue with the same techniques until such time as my game in one department or another tends to slip, when I will be forced to look for other techniques in my determination to stay near the top of the game.

Safety play can be a knowledge of angles, with keen eyesight for hitting thin edges at long distance, with cueing ability to play shots at the right strength. My technique at safety play is to keep as much distance between object ball and cue ball as possible, to leave my opponent with the cue ball as close to a cushion as I can possibly leave it, and, most importantly, to leave the object ball in an area where the pocketing of that object ball will be extremely difficult.

## 58A – Safety Play (Black Only – Thin Edge – Black to Win)

If confronted with the situation shown, I will play a thin edge on the black, cutting it to the middle of the top cushion and bringing the cue ball around the angle along the intended path shown for what I consider would be a good safety shot.

In this case I will play a thin edge on the black ball because the cue ball is travelling from the baulk end to the top end with the nap and will not have its path to the black ball influenced by nap restriction, as it would have if going against the nap. The danger aspect of playing to the thin edges of balls any distance away when playing into the nap is that, should the cue ball turn off its course by only a slight degree, it could completely miss the edge of the black ball, and cost you the frame. Striking point above centre at 13.

## 58B –Safety Play
### (Black Only –Thick Contact –Black to Win)

The opposite situation, with the object ball at the bottom end of the table, and the cue ball at the top end of the table. A nasty position at any time. Now I am forced to play into the nap. There is *no way*, on any table, that I will attempt a thin edge contact on to the black ball.

You cannot play half ball shots from this position as both balls will travel approximately the same distance, and you are most likely to bring the black ball around for an easy potting position for your opponent. In most cases when I am forced to play into the nap over the length of the table and cannot pot the black ball, I will look for a shot that can be played using the thick contact on to the black to bring the black ball to my end of the table and leave my cue ball at the opposite end, thereby forcing my opponent to play his next shot with as much distance between the balls as I can manage. I concentrate on getting the black ball as safe as I can to the end cushion, in preference to concentrating on getting the cue ball safe.

By striking the cue ball in this case at 12 o'clock, I will play into the black three-quarters full on the left hand side, doubling the black ball straight down the table at sufficient speed as to leave it as close to the centre of the top cushion (as per path shown) and the cue ball on to the side cushion, along its intended path.

58B

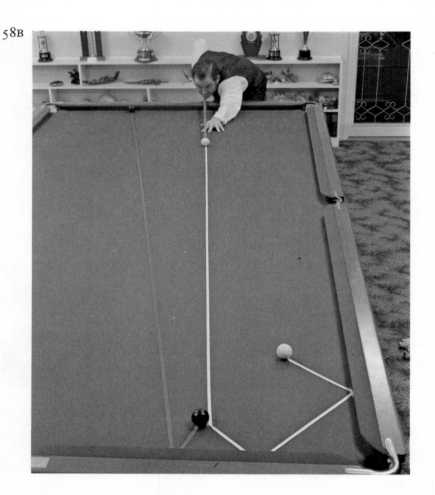

# 59 – Swerve Shot

In playing to swerve the cue ball, raise your cue butt as shown and strike the cue ball on the side of intended swerve. The cue ball struck on the right side curves to the right as it approaches the object ball. The curve of the cue ball is controlled by the striking point on the cue ball, the angle of the cue down on to the cue ball and the power of the shot.

In attempting a swerve shot, your aim at the cue ball is governed by the anticipated curve. When attempting to curve around the blue from position shown to hit the red at the opposite end of the table, I intend to swerve left. My aim is approximately 3" out to the right of the blue ball and, when I strike the cue ball low and left at 7 o'clock at a comfortable speed to reach the red, the cue ball will take the intended arc. In attempting to swerve around the blue ball on the opposite side of the table, the same technique is used but the striking point on the cue ball becomes 5 o'clock. With practice you learn to play this shot at exactly the right speed.

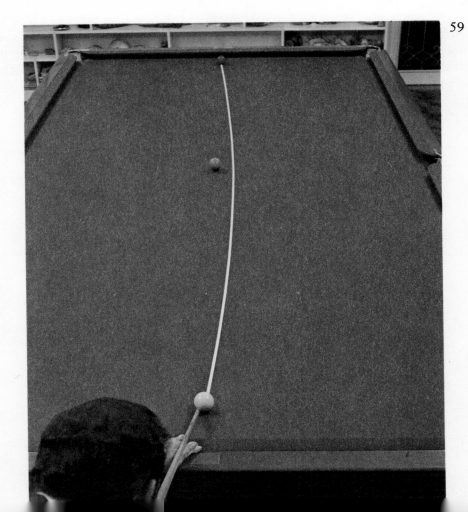

## 60 – Massé Shot

A sharp massé. In setting up to play this shot your stance is upright. Stand as close to and face the table as much as possible. Turn the back of your bridge hand towards the shot. My bridge hand grip is taken on two fingers only and there is a lot of pressure being applied on those fingers to steady my bridge hand for this all important shot.

With my cueing hand, my cue hand grip is taken with the thumb, and first three fingers. My little finger is under the cue butt. Cueing arm is bent as shown and a short grip on cue is a must. Having chalked your tip carefully in attempting one of the most difficult shots in the game and with the cue slanting back against your cheek, play down on the cue ball to massé to the left at 11 o'clock. Do not play through the ball into the cloth as you will only succeed in pushing the cue ball out without getting it back.

A massé is a touch shot where the cue tip must come down briskly to nip down on to the cue ball at 11 o'clock, and up again. Do not play through the ball at all. The cue striking the cue ball at 11 o'clock after having aimed the cue ball safely to the right of the offending object ball or balls will push a little further out to the right of your intended aim in the first instance. The 'push off' of the cue ball from the cue tip becomes spent, and the left hand spin applied viciously by the cue tip nipping on to and off the cue ball, will twist the cue ball to the object ball.

It is extremely important on massé shots to nip the cue ball (11 o'clock) with the right speed. This is a shot which must be practised to bend the path of the cue ball out and back as quickly as intended. To massé the ball the other way, the shot is played the same, however the cue ball is struck on the opposite side (1 o'clock).

Note the bridge hand position for this shot.

# The Rules of Snooker

*The General Rules, when not conflicting with any of the following Rules, govern this Game*

Authorised by The Billiards and Snooker Control Council

DEFINITION
OF GAME

1. The game of SNOOKER (or Snooker's Pool) is played on an English Billiard Table, and may be played by two or more persons, either as sides or independently. It is a game of winning hazards; cannons are ignored. The winner is the player or side making the highest score, or to whom the game under Rule 14 is awarded.

## The Balls

NUMBER
IN SET

2. The set of balls should be twenty-two in number, consisting of fifteen reds, one black, one pink, one blue, one brown, one green, one yellow, and a white ball, which is called the cue ball. In the game on the B. & S.C.C. 6' Standard Table the set of balls shall be seventeen in number, consisting of ten reds, one black, one pink, one blue, one brown, one green, one yellow, and a white ball, which is called the cue ball

## Technical Terms

3. (a) The white ball is referred to as the *cue ball;* the yellow, green, brown, blue, pink and black, as the *pool balls,* or *colours;* the red (or pyramid) balls, as *reds.*

BALL FORCED
OFF TABLE

(b) Any ball which is forced off the table becomes out of play, but, with the exception of a red ball, is immediately replaced upon its allotted spot.

BALL 'ON'.
TO PLAY
AT BALLS

(c) A player is said to be *on* a ball when such ball may be lawfully struck by the cue ball under these Rules. He is *on* a pool ball nominated under Rules 5 and 10.

PLAYER
SNOOKERED

(d) A player is said to be *snookered* with regard to any ball when a direct stroke in a straight line of the cue ball to any point of such ball is obstructed by any ball which is not *on*. If a player is *in hand* after a foul, he cannot be *snookered* with regard to any ball that is *on,* if he can get a direct stroke in a straight line from some part of the 'D' (*i.e.,* a clear ball).

When the ball *on* is snookered by more than one ball, the effective snookering ball is the one nearest to the cue ball.

CUE BALL
ANGLED

(e) The cue ball is said to be *angled* when the corner of the cushion prevents a stroke being made, in a straight line, directly on any part of all balls that may be lawfully struck.

NOMINATED
BALL

(f) A *Nominated Ball* is the object ball which the striker declares he undertakes to strike with the first impact of the cue ball.

PLACING
THE BALLS

4. Fifteen reds in the form of a triangle, the ball at the apex standing as near to the pink ball as possible, without touching it; the base being parallel with and nearest to the top cushion: BLACK on the BILLIARD SPOT; PINK on the PYRAMID SPOT; BLUE on the CENTRE SPOT; BROWN on the MIDDLE of the Baulk-line; GREEN on the LEFT-HAND and YELLOW on the RIGHT-HAND corner of the 'D'.

MODE OF
PLAY

FIRST
STROKE

5. Players must first determine by lot, or other convenient method, the order of their turn, which must remain unaltered throughout the game. The first player shall play from hand. The cue ball shall strike a red as the initial stroke of each turn, until all the reds are off the table. The value of each red, lawfully pocketed by the same stroke, is scored. For the next stroke of the turn (if a score is made) the cue ball shall strike a pool ball, the value of which (if lawfully pocketed) is scored. The game is continued by pocketing reds, and pool balls, alternately, in the same turn. If the striker fails to score, the player next in turn

CUE BALL
POCKETED

plays from where the cue ball came to rest. If the cue ball is pocketed or forced off the table, the next player plays from hand. Once the cue ball has come to rest on the table after a foul has been committed it must be played from where it has come to rest. Each *pool ball* pocketed or forced off

RE-SPOTTING
THE BALLS

the table, must be re-spotted before the next stroke, until finally pocketed under these' Rules. If the player who lawfully pockets the last red, pocket any pool ball with his next

LAST RED
POCKETING

stroke, this ball is re-spotted. Otherwise (reds being off the table) the pool balls must be struck by the cue ball in the progressive order of their values, and *if lawfully pocketed*

POOL BALLS
NOMINATING
INTENTIONAL
MISS

FIRST
IMPACT

are not re-spotted. When requested by the referee a player must state which ball he is *on*. He is advised to do so for his own protection. An intentional miss shall not be made. The player shall, to the best of his ability, endeavour to strike a ball that is *on*.

The first impact of the cue ball shall govern all strokes.

EXAMPLE. A player *on* blue makes the first impact with the cue ball on the blue, the cue ball then strikes the black or any other ball and goes into a pocket, the player is penalised five points, the value of the blue, the ball on which the cue ball made the first impact.

6. The scoring values of the balls are: red=1, yellow=2, green=3, brown=4, blue=5, pink=6, black=7.

7. The striker must see that every ball required to be re-spotted is properly placed before he plays his stroke. *Reds* are never re-spotted. Any pool ball pocketed by a foul stroke is not deemed to have been lawfully pocketed, and shall be re-spotted. If the spot, named in Rule 4 for each pool ball, is occupied when such ball shall be placed thereon, the ball shall be placed on the spot first named in Rule 4, that is then unoccupied, *i.e.*, if the spot allocated to the yellow is occupied by another ball, after the yellow has been pocketed, then the yellow ball is to be placed on the black spot, or, if that is occupied, then on the pink spot, and so on. If all the spots are occupied, any pool ball other than the black and pink shall be placed as near its own spot as possible between that spot and the *nearest part* of the top cushion without touching another ball. In the case of the black and pink balls being potted and all the spots are occupied, they shall be placed as near as possible to their own spots, up the table, on the centre line of the table, and without touching another ball. If the space between the black spot and the top cushion is occupied, the black ball shall be placed as near as possible to the black spot, on the centre line of the table, below its spot, and without touching another ball. Similarly if the space between the pink spot and the top cushion is occupied, the pink shall be placed as near as possible to the pink spot, on the centre line of the table, below its spot, and without touching another ball.

| | | |
|---|---|---|
| BALLS STRUCK SIMULTANEOUSLY OR POCKETED IN ONE STROKE | 8. | Two balls (other than two reds or the ball *on* and the ball nominated under Rule 10) must not be struck simultaneously nor pocketed by the same stroke.<br><br>NOTE: Any number of red balls may be pocketed by one stroke made in accordance with these rules. |

CUE BALL TOUCHING   9. (a) If the cue ball is touching another ball which is *on*, the striker must play away from the touching ball without moving the latter, or he must be held to have pushed. The striker thus playing away from a ball *on* shall incur no penalty for a miss or for striking another ball, but he may lawfully pocket any other ball which is *on*. If he pockets a ball which is not *on*, he forfeits the penalty under Rule 12.

(b) If the cue ball is touching another ball which is not *on*, the striker must play away from such ball as in (a). If the ball *on* is missed, or another ball hit, the penalty as laid down in Rule 12 must be forfeited.

(c) In all cases where the cue ball is touching the ball *on* or touching a colour after a red has been potted, the referee shall state 'TOUCHING BALL' without being asked. If the cue ball is touching more than one ball *on* he shall, on request, state which ball(s) the cue ball is touching. He shall offer no other information.

EXAMPLES: (1) The *ball on is red*, cue ball is *touching red*, striker plays away from red without disturbing it, strikes and goes in off black. The penalty is four points, the value of the ball *on*.

(2) The *ball on is yellow*, cue ball is *touching yellow*, striker plays away from yellow without disturbing it, and pockets black. The penalty is seven points, the value of the ball *pocketed*.

(3) The *ball on is red*, cue ball is *touching black*, striker plays away from black without disturbing it, misses all balls and cue ball enters a pocket. The penalty is four points, the value of the ball *on*.

(4) In the case of the striker, playing away from black, missing all reds and striking blue he is penalised five points.

SNOOKERING AFTER 10. After a foul stroke, if the striker be snookered, (a) *with re-*
A FOUL *gard to all reds*, he is then *on* any ball he may nominate, and for all purposes such nominated ball shall be regarded as a red, except that, if pocketed, it shall be spotted.

(b) After a foul stroke, if the striker be snookered (*reds being off the table*), *with regard to the pool ball on,* he is then *on* any ball he may nominate, and for all purposes such nominated ball shall be regarded as the ball *on*, except that should it be lawfully pocketed it shall be spotted, and the player shall continue his break on the ball he was *on*, but for being snookered. If, as a result of playing on the nominated ball, the ball *on* be pocketed, it shall be scored and

the player continues his break. Should both the nominated ball and the ball *on* be pocketed by the same stroke, only the ball *on* shall be scored, and the player continues his break. The nominated ball only shall be re-spotted.

Should the striker leave the opponent snookered by the nominated ball it is a foul stroke, except when only pink and black remain on the table.

Should the striker fail to hit the ball nominated under this Rule it is a foul stroke.

11. If the cue ball is angled it must be played from where it lies; but if angled after a foul, it may be played from hand, at the striker's discretion.

12. A player who contravenes any Rule of this game (a) cannot score; (b) loses his turn; (c) forfeits such points as are exacted in these Rules – which are added to his opponent's score; (d) in addition, the striker has the option of playing from where the balls have come to rest, or requesting the opponent to play the stroke; (e) minimum penalty for any infringement is four points.

13. The player contravenes these rules by the following acts (among others): –
    (a) By making a losing hazard. Penalty, value of ball *on*, or value of ball struck, whichever is the higher.
    (b) By causing the cue ball to strike a ball he is not *on*. Penalty, value of the ball struck, or value of the ball *on*, whichever is the higher.
    (c) By making a miss. Penalty, value of ball *on*.
    (d) By snookering his opponent with the nominated ball after a foul stroke, except when only pink and black remain. Penalty, value of the ball *on*.
    (e) By striking simultaneously or pocketing with one stroke two balls, except two reds, or the ball *on* and the ball nominated. Penalty, highest value of the two struck, or pocketed.

(f)    By moving an object ball in contravention of Rule 9 (Cue ball Touching). Penalty, value of the ball *on*, or value of the ball moved, whichever is the higher.

(g)    By forcing a ball off the table. Penalty, the value of the ball *on* or the value of the ball forced off the table, whichever is the higher.

(h)    By pocketing any ball not *on*. Penalty, value of the ball pocketed, or value of the ball *on*, whichever is the higher.

(i)    For playing with other than the cue ball. Penalty, seven points.

(j)    By playing at two reds in successive strokes. Penalty, seven points.

(k)    By using a dead ball to test whether a ball will pass another, or go on a spot, or for any other purpose. Penalty, seven points.

(l)    By playing with both feet off the floor. Penalty – value of the ball *on*, or value of the ball struck, or value of the ball pocketed or value of the ball improperly spotted, whichever is the higher.

(m)    By playing before the balls have come to rest, or before they have been spotted or when wrongly spotted. Penalty, value of the ball *on*, or value of the ball struck, or value of the ball wrongly spotted, or value of the ball pocketed, whichever is the higher.

(n)    By striking or touching a ball whilst in play, otherwise than with the tip of the cue. Penalty, value of the *ball struck* or *touched,* or value of the ball *on,* whichever is the higher.

(o)    By playing improperly from hand. Penalty, value of the ball *on*, or value of the ball struck, or value of the ball pocketed, or value of the ball improperly spotted, whichever is the higher.

(p)    Push Stroke. Penalty, value of the ball *on*, or value of the ball struck, or value of the ball pocketed, whichever is the higher.

(q)    Jump Shot. Penalty, value of the ball *on,* or value of the ball struck, or value of the ball pocketed, whichever is the higher.

(r)    By playing out of turn. Penalty, value of the ball *on,* or value of the ball struck, or value of the ball pocketed, whichever is the higher.

Only the referee is allowed to clean a ball on the table. He should do so at a player's request.

It is the striker's responsibility to see that the balls are correctly spotted before playing his stroke.

If the referee considers that a player is taking an abnormal amount of time over his stroke, with the intention of upsetting his opponent, the referee should warn him that he runs the risk of being disqualified if he pursues these tactics.

A player should not be penalised if, when using the rest, the rest head falls off and touches a ball.

Unless a foul stroke is awarded by the referee, or claimed by the non-striker, before the next stroke is made, it is condoned.

If the striker plays with the balls improperly spotted, he scores all points made until the foul is awarded by the referee, or claimed by the non-striker.

The referee should not give any indication that a player is about to make a foul stroke.

If the striker makes a miss, the referee can order him to replay the stroke penalising him the requisite forfeit for each miss, but he scores all points in any subsequent stroke.

When awarded a free ball a player need only nominate the ball he intends to play, when requested to do so by the referee.

If at the opening stroke of a game the striker fails to hit a red, the next player plays from where the cue ball has come to rest .

**A SNOOKER**

A player must be able to strike both sides of the ball *on* free of obstruction from any ball or balls not *on*. It virtually means the diameter of a ball on either side of the ball *on*.

If a player is colour blind, the referee should tell him the colour of a ball if requested.

A referee must declare when a player has a free ball without appeal from a player.

**EXAMPLES OF FOUL STROKES**

EXAMPLES: (1) *Red is the ball on,* striker fouls *the black* with his cue or otherwise, the penalty is seven points, the value of the *ball fouled.*

(2) *Black is the ball on,* striker fouls *a red* with his cue or arm, the penalty is seven points, the value of the *ball on.*

(3) A player pots the *pink* and before it is properly spotted he pots a *red* ball – what is the penalty?

Decision: 6 points for playing with the balls not properly spotted (value of the ball not properly spotted).

| | |
|---|---|
| WILFUL EVASION OF SPIRIT OF RULES | If a game is awarded to a player under Rule 15 GENERAL RULES, the offender shall lose the game, and forfeit all points he may have scored, or the value of the balls on the table (red = 8 each) whichever is higher. |
| END OF GAME AND TIE | 14. When only the black ball is left, the first score or forfeit ends the game, unless the scores are then equal, in which case the black is spotted, and the players draw lots for choice of playing at the black from hand. The next score or forfeit ends the game. In games (whether individuals, pairs or teams) where aggregate points decide the winner, it is only when the scores are equal **as a result of the last frame,** that the black is re-spotted. The next score or forfeit ends the game. |
| FOUR-HANDED SNOOKER | Rules of Snooker apply. |
| | In a four-handed match at snooker whether it be on frames or on aggregate points, each side shall open alternative frames, but the order of play shall be determined at the commencement of each frame. Players may change order of play at the beginning of each frame which must be maintained throughout that frame. |
| | If a foul is committed and a request is made to play again, the player who committed the foul plays again, and the order of play is maintained. |
| | When a game ends in a tie Snooker Rule 14 is applied. The pair who play the first stroke have the choice as to which player plays that stroke. The order of play must be maintained as in the frame. |

# General Rules

*These General Rules, Technical Terms and Laws apply to Games played on an English Billiard Table*

Authorised by The Billiards and Snooker Control Council

## *The Table*

| | |
|---|---|
| MEASUREMENTS | 1. The B. & S.C.C. 12 ft. Standard Table: The slate bed of the table shall measure 12 ft. by 6 ft. 1½ in. The edge of the cushions shall not project over the slate more than |
| HEIGHT | 2 in. or less than 1½ in. The height of the table, from the floor to the top of the cushion rail, shall be from 2 ft. 9½ in. to 2 ft. 10½ in. There shall be pockets at the corners |

(the two at the Baulk end being known as the bottom pockets and the two at the spot end as the top pockets) and at the middle of the longer sides, and the pocket opening shall conform to the templates authorised by The Billiards and Snooker Control Council.

A straight line drawn 29 inches from the face of the bottom cushion and parallel to it is called the Baulk-line, and the intervening space is termed the Baulk. The 'D' is a semi-circle described in baulk, with its centre at the middle of the baulk-line, and with a radius of 11 ½ inches.

Spots MARKED on the table are:

(a) THE SPOT, 12¾ inches from a point perpendicular below the face of the top cushion on the centre longitudinal line of the table;

(b) THE CENTRE SPOT, mid-way between the middle pockets;

(c) THE PYRAMID SPOT, mid-way between the CENTRE SPOT and the face of the top cushion; and

(d) THE MIDDLE OF THE BAULK-LINE — all four being on the centre longitudinal line of the table.

1. (a) The B. & S.C.C. 6 ft. Standard Table.—The slate bed of the table shall be not less than ½ in. in thickness and shall measure 6 ft. by 3 ft. 1½ in. The edge of the cushions shall project over the slate 1½ in. There shall be pockets at the corners and at the middle of the long sides, and the pocket openings shall conform to the templates authorised by The Billiards and Snooker Control Council for 6 ft. standard tables.

A straight line drawn 14½ inches from the face of the bottom cushion and parallel to it is called the Baulk-line, and the intervening space is termed the Baulk. The 'D' is a semi-circle described in Baulk, with its centre at the middle of the Baulk-line and with a radius of 5¾ inches.

Spots MARKED on the table are:

(a) THE SPOT, 7 inches from a point perpendicular below the face of the top cushion on the centre longitudinal line of the table;

(b) THE CENTRE SPOT, mid-way between the middle pockets;

(c) THE PYRAMID SPOT, mid-way between the CENTRE SPOT and the face of the top cushion; and

(d) THE MIDDLE OF THE BAULK-LINE—all four being on the centre longitudinal line of the table.

## Balls

MEASUREMENTS

2. The B. & S.C.C. 12 ft. Standard Table balls should be of equal size and weight, and of a diameter of $2^1/_{16}$ inches, within manufacturers' tolerance.

The B. & S.C.C. 6 ft. Standard Table balls should be of equal size and weight, and of a diameter of $1^7/_8$ inches, within manufacturers' tolerance.

## The Cue

2. (a) A Billiard Cue as recognised by the B. & S. C.C. shall be not less than three feet in length and shall show no substantial departure from the traditional and generally accepted shape and form.

## Technical Terms

TO STRING

3. (a) To string is to play together from the Baulk-line to the top cushion with the object of leaving player's ball as near as possible to the bottom cushion.

CUE BALL

(b) The cue ball is the ball of the striker; all other balls are object balls.

BALL IN HAND

(c) A player's ball is *in hand* when it is off the table.

TO PLAY FROM HAND

(d) To play from hand the striker must play the cue ball from some position on or within the lines of the 'D'.

BALL IN BAULK

(e) A ball is *in baulk* when it rests on the Baulk-line or between that line and the bottom cushion.

BALL OFF THE TABLE

(f) A ball is *forced off the table* which comes to rest otherwise than on the bed of the table or in a pocket.

STRIKER AND NON-STRIKER

(g) The person about to play or in play is termed the *Striker;* his opponent is the *Non-Striker.*

BALL IN PLAY

(h) The ball of the striker is *in play* when it has been finally place on the table and struck with the tip of the cue (or spotted under the Rules of the game being played), and remains so until pocketed. The ball of the non-striker is *in play* when it has been spotted under the Rules of the game being played. Other balls are in play when spotted and remain so until pocketed.

Any ball which is forced off the table becomes out of play.

A STROKE      (i)    A Stroke is made by a player touching his ball, or striking his ball when it is in play, with the tip of his cue. No stroke is completed until all the balls have come to rest and the player is adjudged to have left the table.

A BREAK      (j)    A Break is a series of consecutive scoring strokes made in any one turn.

A CANNON      (k)    A Cannon is made when the striker's ball makes contact with two other balls.

WINNING HAZARD      (l)    A Winning Hazard is made when a ball, other than the cue ball is pocketed after contact with another ball

LOSING HAZARD      (m)    A Losing Hazard is made when the cue ball is pocketed after contact with another ball.

A MISS      (n)    A Miss is a stroke where the cue ball fails to touch any other ball; or in Billiards where the cue ball, when played from hand, strikes any part of a ball in baulk without first hitting a ball or cushion out of baulk; or where the cue ball is struck more than once before contact with another ball.

SPOT OCCUPIED      (o)    A spot or position is said to be *occupied* if a ball cannot be placed thereon without touching or disturbing another ball.

THE FALL      (p)    The curved edge of the bed of the table forming the mouth of the pocket is called the fall.

FIRST IMPACT OF CUE BALL      4.    The first impact of the cue ball shall govern all strokes.

BALL PROPERLY SPOTTED      5.    A ball is not considered to be spotted unless it has been placed by hand on its prescribed spot.

A FAIR STROKE      6.    All strokes must be made with the tip of the cue. The ball must be struck, and not pushed. The ball must not be struck more than once in the same stroke either before or after contact with another ball. At the moment of striking, one of the player's feet must touch the floor. A ball or balls must not be forced off the table.

A FOUL STROKE      7.    A foul stroke is one made in contravention of any Rule of the game being played (see Sectional Rules).

| | | |
|---|---|---|
| BALL ON EDGE OF POCKET | 8. | If the ball which falls is part of the stroke, that stroke shall be void, the balls placed in their original position and the stroke replayed. If the ball is not an integral part of the stroke, the stroke shall stand and the ball which fell only shall be replaced. If it balances momentarily on the edge and fall in, it must not be replaced. |
| BALL MOVED BY OTHER AGENCY THAN PLAYER | 9. | If a ball is disturbed otherwise than by the player, it shall, if moved, be placed on the table by the referee on the spot which, in his judgment, the ball had, or if moving, would have occupied. This rule covers the case in which a non-striker or non-player causes the striker to touch or move a ball. The player shall not be responsible for any disturbance of the balls by the referee or by the marker. |
| CONDUCT OF NON-STRIKER | 10. | The non-striker shall, when the striker is playing, avoid standing or moving in the line of sight; he should sit or stand at a fair distance from the table. He may, in case of his enforced absence from the room, appoint a substitute to watch his interests, and claim a foul if necessary. |
| PENALTIES | 11. | If during a stroke any rule is contravened the striker (a) cannot score, (b) loses his turn, (c) forfeits such points as are exacted under the Rules of the game being played. |
| BALLS CHANGED | 12. | The set of balls may be changed during a game, by consent of the players or by decision of the referee. |
| ORDER OF TURN

COMMENCEMENT OF GAME | 13. | The players shall determine the order of play by stringing or by lot; the order of play shall remain unaltered throughout the game. The game does not commence until the cue ball has been finally placed on the table and struck with the tip of the cue, by the first player. |
| THE REFEREE | 14. | (a) The Referee shall be the sole judge of fair or unfair play, and shall be responsible for the proper conduct of the game under these Rules, and shall, of his own initiative, intervene if he sees any contravention. He shall, on appeal by a player, and on appeal only, decide any question of fact connected with play. (The referee on appeal if a ball is in or out of baulk shall only give a decision when the player is in hand.)

(EXAMPLES: If a ball touch the striker's ball; if it is properly placed to play from hand; or if properly spotted.)

If he has failed to observe any incident, he may take the evidence of the spectators best placed for observation, to assist his decision. |

He shall decide all questions arising between the players on the interpretations of these rules.

The referee shall not give any advice or express opinion on points affecting play.

(EXAMPLES: The referee should not offer an opinion as to whether there is room for a ball to be spotted if pocketed by a stroke about to be played. If the striker plays from hand outside the limits of the 'D', the referee shall not warn him before the stroke is played, but shall award the foul immediately afterwards.)

THE MARKER 14. (b) The Marker shall keep the score on the marking board, and assist the referee to carry out his duties.

PLAYER'S CONDUCT 15. For refusing to continue the game when called upon by the referee to do so, or for conduct which, in the opinion of the referee, is wilfully or persistently unfair, a player shall lose the game, and is liable to be disqualified for any future competition held under the control of The Billiards Association and Control Council, or its Affiliated Associations.

THE SPECTATORS 16. Spectators should not interfere with the game, the players, the marker, or the referee.

THE PUSH STROKE A Push Stroke is a foul and is made when (A) the tip of the cue remains in contact with the cue ball when the cue ball makes contact with the object ball, or when (B) the tip of the cue remains in contact with the cue ball after the cue ball has commenced its forward motion. Penalty in Billiards: None. In conjunction with a miss one away. In Snooker: Value of the ball 'on', or value of the ball struck, or value of the ball pocketed, whichever is the higher.

THE JUMP SHOT The Jump Shot is a foul in which the cue ball is made to jump over any ball whether by accident or design. Penalty in Billiards: None. In conjunction with a miss, one away. In Snooker: Value of the ball 'on', or value of the ball struck, or value of the ball pocketed, whichever is the higher.

# List of Lessons